Jesus 4U!

Quick Elementary Bible Lessons
to Pick Up 'n' Do!

by Lois Keffer
and Mary Grace Becker

NEXGEN®

Building the New Generation of Believers

An Imprint of Cook Communications Ministries
Colorado Springs, Colorado

Just Add Kids Jesus 4U!
Copyright © 2004 Cook Communications Ministries

All rights reserved. No part of this book may be reproduced in any manner whatsoever without prior
written permission from the publisher, except where noted on handouts and the case of brief quotations embodied in critical articles and reviews. For information write to Permissions Editor, Cook
Communications Ministries, 4050 Lee Vance View, Colorado Springs, Colorado 80918.

Scripture quotations, unless otherwise noted, are from

THE HOLY BIBLE, NEW INTERNATIONAL VERSION (NIV)
Copyright © 1973, 1978, 1984 by International Bible Society.
Used by permission of Zondervan Publishing House. All rights reserved.

Written and edited by: Mary Grace Becker, Lois Keffer
Art Direction: Nancy L. Haskins
Cover Design: Helen Harrison
Interior Design: Nancy L. Haskins, Helen Harrison, Lois Keffer
Illustrators: Kris and Sharon Cartwright and Lois Keffer

Printed in the United States

First printing, 2004
1 2 3 4 5 6 7 8 9 10   06 05 04

ISBN 0781440696

Table of Contents

Quick Start Guide

Just Add Kids! elementary lessons give your kids great Bible teaching and serious discipleship without hours of preparation. You and your kids will love these large group/small group lessons. Two options let you take the lesson from super simple to more challenging.

If you're looking for an "instant" lesson that you can pick up and do at the last minute, you've got it in Bible 4U! and Shepherd's Spot.

All you need is a photocopier and basic classroom supplies such as pencils, scissors and glue sticks. Copy the **Bible 4U!** instant drama and the **Shepherd's Spot** handout and you're ready to go.

Are you looking for something beyond the basics?

The optional **Get Set** section of the lessons gives you an opportunity to get a puppet into the action. "Schooner" is a mouthy macaw whose bright remarks will bring giggles and grins each week. And he does a smack up job of setting up the Bible story.

Don't have a puppet ministry team in your church? How about recruiting middle schoolers? The lively back and forth between Schooner and the Leader is right up their alley. What a great way to get them involved in ministry to younger children!

Now for the heart of the lesson

Bible 4U!

The Bible is full of drama! What better way to teach than with fascinating dramas that take a unique approach to each Bible story. Photocopy the instant drama, pull volunteers from your group to read the roles and you're ready to go.

You'll keep your knowledgeable students engaged, and give kids who are new to God's Word a solid foundation of Biblical truth. The dramas call for just a few characters. You may want to play the main role yourself. Or, call on a teen or adult drama troupe to prepare and present the dramas each week. Either way, kids will see the Bible stories come to life in unforgettable ways.

1.
Bible 4U!

Shepherd's Spot

This is the second essential step of the lesson. After **Bible 4U!**, kids break into small groups with one adult helper for every eight to ten kids. Nothing leaves a more indelible impact on kids' lives than the warm, personal touch of a caring adult. The photocopiable instructions and handouts will give your helpers the confidence they need to help kids consider how to live out what they've learned.

In the **Shepherd's Spot**, kids will read the story straight from the Bible. They'll learn basic Bible skills, and complete a fun, photocopiable handout that helps them understand how to get the story off the page and into their lives. They'll close each week by sharing concerns and praying together.

2.
Shepherd's
Spot

Workshop Wonders

And there's more! Each week, the optional **Workshop Wonders** section gives you a game, craft, science or cooking activity that gets your kids out of their chairs and into the action.

The **Workshop Wonders** activities require more than the usual classroom supplies. If you choose one of these activities, you'll need to pick up cooking or science ingredients or a few simple craft or game supplies. If you don't mind a little extra preparation, you'll find that there's nothing like a little hands-on action to bring that moment of learning wonder to kids' faces.

These special activities are guaranteed to make a memory and help the Bible lesson stick with kids for a long time to come.

That's it! You can go for a quick, simple lesson with **Bible 4U!** and the **Shepherd's Spot**.

If you wish, add another level of excitement and learning with the Schooner script in the optional Get Set section of each lesson.

And if you love teaching with activities, do a little shopping and give kids the memorable experiences of **Workshop Wonders**.

Do you want to give your kids even more great stuff?

How About Staff?

Finding Schooner

If you do the **Get Set** option to open the lessons, you'll want to purchase a parrot or scarlet macaw puppet.

You'll find a great selection on the Internet, in all sizes and prices. Type "scarlet macaw puppet" into your favorite search engine and browse until you find the puppet that suits your price range.

You need just a few helpers to make Just Add Kids lessons a great experience for you and your kids!

1. A leader/emcee hosts the **Bible 4U!** instant drama each week. For a quick presentation, pull kids from your group to read the roles in the dramas. When there are just one or two parts, you may want to step into the leading role yourself.

2. You may wish to ask a small drama troupe to prepare the stories each week. Five or six volunteers who serve on a rotating basis can easily cover the stories with just a few minutes' preparation.

3. For the **Shepherd's Spot,** you'll need one adult leader for every eight to ten kids. You'll need caring adults in this role—people who are good listeners and feel comfortable sharing their lives with kids. This is a great first step into children's ministry for adults who haven't taught before.

4. If you choose to do the optional **Get Set** puppet script, you'll need a leader and a puppeteer. It's best to use the same leader who hosts the Bible dramas. If you recruit a couple of people to play Schooner, they can rotate every few weeks.

For Overachievers

Do you have a great stage set-up at your church? Then you may want to go for some flash and glitz. Give Schooner a little tropical cabana with a palm tree and a sea-breezy backdrop. Make sure your leader has an obnoxious tropical shirt to slip on.

Don't forget the music! Warm kids up each week with lively, interactive praise songs. Then bring on Schooner's set to the tune of island rhythms.

Equip your drama troupe with a box full of Bibletime costumes. You'll find tips for props and staging in the "for Overachievers" box just before each Bible story. Of course, all this pizzazz is purely optional. The most important ingredient in a wonderful Bible lesson is YOU—the warm, caring leader whose love for kids calls you into children's ministry in the first place! There is absolutely no substitute for the personal attention you give to children each week. You become the model of Jesus himself through your gifts of time and commitment.

God bless you as you minister to his kids!

Follow that Star!

Get Set

Option

LARGE GROUP ■ Greet kids and do a puppet skit. Schooner finds out why we give gifts at Christmas.

❏ large bird puppet ❏ puppeteer

Bible 4U! Instant Drama

1

LARGE GROUP ■ Three wise men on a mission share their adventure and discovery.

❏ 3 actors ❏ copies of pp. 10-11, Mystery Men from the East script
❏ 4 numbered balls Optional: ❏ 3 dust mops ❏ rich-looking fabrics for costumes

Shepherd's Spot

2

SMALL GROUP ■ Use the "Starlight, Star Bright" handout to help kids discover how they can worship Jesus.

❏ Bibles ❏ pencils ❏ scissors ❏ copies of p. 14, Starlight, Star Bright
❏ copies p. 16, Special Delivery

Workshop Wonders

Option

SMALL GROUP ■ Mix and roll fragrant ornaments as reminders of the rich gifts the wise men gave Jesus when they worshiped him.

❏ bowl ❏ rolling pin ❏ ground cinnamon, cloves, nutmeg and ginger
❏ drained applesauce ❏ white glue ❏ Christmas cookie cutters ❏ ribbon
❏ toothpick Optional: ❏ waxed paper ❏ envelopes ❏ cinnamon sticks

Bible Basis—
Jesus is born.
Matthew 2:1–12

Learn It!
God sent his
Son for us.

Live It!
Worship
Jesus!

Bible Verse
Glory to God in the highest, and on earth peace to men on whom his favor rests. Luke 2:14

Matthew 2:1-12

After Jesus was born in Bethlehem in Judea, during the time of King Herod, Magi from the east came to Jerusalem 2 and asked, "Where is the one who has been born king of the Jews? We saw his star in the east and have come to worship him." 3 When King Herod heard this he was disturbed, and all Jerusalem with him. 4 When he had called together all the people's chief priests and teachers of the law, he asked them where the Christ was to be born. 5 "In Bethlehem in Judea," they replied, "for this is what the prophet has written: 6 "'But you, Bethlehem, in the land of Judah, are by no means least among the rulers of Judah; for out of you will come a ruler who will be the shepherd of my people Israel.'" 7 Then Herod called the Magi secretly and found out from them the exact time the star had appeared.

8 He sent them to Bethlehem and said, "Go and make a careful search for the child. As soon as you find him, report to me, so that I too may go and worship him." 9 After they had heard the king, they went on their way, and the star they had seen in the east went ahead of them until it stopped over the place where the child was. 10 When they saw the star, they were overjoyed. 11 On coming to the house, they saw the child with his mother Mary, and they bowed down and worshiped him. Then they opened their treasures and presented him with gifts of gold and of incense and of myrrh. 12 And having been warned in a dream not to go back to Herod, they returned to their country by another route.

Insights

Magi from the east—the very phrase conjures mystery. And they are a mystery! Where were they from? Persia seems a likely guess, but it's just a guess. When Jerusalem fell in 537 BC, the Jews were exiled to locations all over the Babylonian empire. When King Nebuchadnezzar allowed the return of the exiles, many Jews chose to remain in the countries where they'd settled. This left pockets of Jewish communities all around the known world.

Perhaps interaction with such a community allowed the Gentile wise men to discover the prophecies of the Messiah. The wise men may have been political advisors, who studied philosophy, religion, astronomy and interpreted dreams, much like the wise men mentioned in the book of Daniel.

Were there three? We know only that there was more than one, and that they presented three gifts. Ancient mosaics show anywhere from two to eight. They were men of means: they could afford a lengthy journey and offer costly gifts. And being wealthy, they probably traveled on fine horses rather than camels!

The scant information Scripture gives us about the wise men leaves all of these things open to conjecture. But there's one fact that is clear as a starlit Christmas night—God touched the hearts of these Gentiles and inspired them to seek out and worship the child Jesus. He spoke to them through the Scriptures, through a dream, and through a star that didn't behave as stars usually do.

As you teach this lesson, pray that God will use it to inspire the hearts of your children to seek and worship the infant savior. Perhaps this will be the day they acknowledge his lordship and present him with the rich gift of their hearts.

Option Get Set

Open with live praise songs, then greet the kids. **There are a lot of cool things about Christmas, but one of them is that you can celebrate it any time of year. Like today! We've got a little Christmas in the air.** *Schooner pops up.*

Schooner: Hi, boss.

Leader: Hello, Schooner. You're looking good today.

Schooner: *(preening feathers)* I'm having my picture taken.

Leader: What's the occasion?

Schooner: Every Christmas Grandma Screech puts out the call—caw, caw, caw—for all the kids to come back to the nest.

Leader: A Christmas family reunion?

Schooner: Yup. And we always do a family portrait. We polish our beaks, fluff our feathers, hop on the Christmas tree and say cheese.

Leader: I didn't know you liked cheese.

Schooner: I don't. But where there's cheese, there are crackers.

Leader: As in Polly want a…

Schooner: Don't even think about going there.

Leader: Sorry. So, do you have a nice collection of parrot portraits?

Schooner: You bet. Birds of a feather perched all over the tree. *(sobs)* It's so beautiful…

Leader: Don't get mushy on me, Schooner.

Schooner: *big sniff; wipes his beak on Leader's shoulder*

Leader: That was tweet of you.

Schooner: Don't mention it.

Leader: I already did. Do you have a collection of the parrot family Christmas pictures from each year?

Schooner: Oh yeah. The first pictures were taken when I was a little squawker just barely able to wing it.

Leader: Has the family grown a lot since then?

Schooner: I'll say. We have to get a bigger tree each year so there's a branch for everybody.

Leader: Pictures are a nice way to keep track of everyone. Kind of like a census.

Schooner: A cen…what?

Leader: A census. Back in Bible times the Romans kept track of everyone with a census.

Schooner: Sounds fun. Did they take pictures?

Leader: No pictures, and not very much fun. They counted people and made them pay taxes.

Schooner: Taxes? Like money to pay for the government and soldiers and stuff?

Leader: Exactly. Everybody had to travel back to their home town to pay up.

Schooner: Bummer. Less money to spend on Christmas presents.

Leader: Christmas presents hadn't been invented yet.

Schooner: *(gasps)* I didn't know there was ever a time without Christmas presents. Whoa, I'm glad I live now instead of then.

Leader: Do you know who started the whole thing with Christmas presents?

Schooner: *(cocks head to the side)* Uh, well, uh…

Leader: Let me give you some hints: they were really wise and they followed a star.

Schooner: Um, astronauts?

Leader: Wrong! Sounds like you have a few things to learn from today's Bible story.

Schooner: So what are we waiting for?

Leader: You to get off the stage.

Schooner: I'm outta' here, I'm outta here!

Leader: Okay—here's Bible 4U!

1 Bible 4U!

Have the three kings and the star wait out of sight. **Welcome to Bible 4U! Theater—where Bible stories come to life before your very eyes!** Actually, I'm kind of embarrassed about today's story because our Bible characters are kind of, you know...lost. They set out on an important mission and things went very well for them at first, but now you might say their prospects for the future are a little up in the air.

Instant Prep

Before class, ask three volunteers who are good readers to play the roles of the Wise Men. You can use both girls and boys. Give them copies of the "Starlight, Star Bright" script below. You'll need a fourth silent volunteer to play the star and "twinkle" with the audience.

for Overachievers

Have a four-person drama team prepare the story. Gather rich-looking fabrics for the wise men to wear as shawls and headpieces. Dress the star in white with a glitter garland and sheer white scarves or fabric tied to the wrists. Give the wise men dust mops to "ride."

There's another thing that's strange about this story: our three characters play an important role in the Bible, but we don't know their names. Their background is a mystery—all we know about them is that they were wealthy and wise, and came from a mysterious country in the East. They're headed for a date with destiny, but they don't know where and they don't know when. The year is 1 AD. The place is near the city of Jerusalem. It's nighttime. Let's check in with our mystery men and see where their quest leads them.

Starlight, Star Bright
Based on Matthew 2:1–12

Three wise men enter, peering up and out over the audience.

King 1: Stargazing again?

King 2: I wish! We lost it. It's not there. Not a twinkle or a glimmer. Our star has simply disappeared.

King 1: I know. I can't believe it. After all these weeks of following, following...it just goes out.

King 3: Is that why you were up six times last night, pacing around the tent and squinting at the sky?

King 2: I don't squint. I look intently. And I was only up five times.

King 3: Excuse me. Is that why you were up five times last night looking intently at the sky?

King 1: Well, can you blame him? We haven't seen it for three nights.

King 3: Don't worry. This road trip wasn't our idea. Remember when we saw the star for the first time?

King 2: Oh, yeah! It was like God whispered to us, "Go find the special child who will be king."

King 3: Have faith then! God is the one who sets the stars in space.

King 2: We've had some cloudy nights, that's all.

King 1: Yeah, ever since we stopped by Jerusalem and talked to King Herod. *(shudders)*

King 2: Oh, man. I'm with you there. He was one creepy guy.

King 3: It was pretty obvious that he didn't want any kings around here but him.

King 1: He didn't do a very good job of hiding how he felt about another king being born.

King 2: He really didn't. I'll bet Herod can get pretty nasty when things don't go his way.

King 3: The king we're looking for won't be anything like that. He will be wise and kind and rule over many nations…a king such as the world has never seen before.

King 1: A king who truly deserves our worship and the rich gifts we bring.

King 2: If we find him. Where is that star?

King 3: It will appear—have faith. God has brought us this far. He won't leave us now.

King 2: I'm glad you're so sure. I'm beginning to…hey, wait! *(looks out over the audience)*

King 3: What? What?

King 1: Look! *(points)* It's starting to clear up. The clouds are moving out and…

All 3: There's our star!

A fourth volunteer enters from the back, dances to the front of the room with fingers "twinkling," then exits. Everyone gives high fives and calls out "Woohoo!"

King 1: Oh, man, that's a relief.

King 2: No kidding.

King 3: It was never in doubt. And look—the star is leading us right to Bethlehem, the place the Scriptures said the king would be born.

King 1: Well, let's not stand here talking about it. Mount up!

The three kings pantomime riding in a circle, then come back around to face the audience. They kneel and hold out their hands as if they're presenting gifts. Then they rise, ride their imaginary camels in a circle, and face the audience again.

King 3: I will never forget this day.

King 1: The tiny king, Jesus, is God's own Son.

King 2: Itty-bitty hands, itty-bitty feet…

King 1: And a heart as big as the whole world.

King 3: Isn't it amazing that God chose us to find his star?

King 2: And warned us away from King Herod?

King 1: And let us see the Son of God with our own eyes?

King 2: Jesus is a king, not just for our time, but for all time.

King 3: Thousands of years in the future, parents will tell their children about the king we worshiped.

King 1: And children will learn about him in Sunday school.

King 2: What's Sunday school?

King 1: I'm not sure—it hasn't been invented yet.

King 3: Well, boys, it's a long way home.

King 2: *(rubs his backside)* I'm not sure I'm ready to get on that camel again.

King 1: No whining. Absolutely no whining!

King 2: Not even one or two, "Are we there yets?"

Kings 1 & 3: NO!

King 2: Fine…fine, fine, FINE!

King 3: Mount up. *(points)* To the east! Giddyup!

They "ride off" singing "We Three Kings."

And they're off! Riding into the sunrise, mission accomplished. The wise men went out of their way to worship Jesus and celebrate his coming into the world. Let's see if you know why. Toss the four numbered balls to different parts of the room.

Bring the kids with the balls to the front one by one and ask these questions. Allow kids to get help from the group if they need it. After each correct answer, let kids drop the ball into a bag.

 ■ **Why did the wise men go to all the trouble of finding baby Jesus?**

 ■ **If the wise men were to come here today, what questions would you ask them?**

 ■ **How do you think they would answer those questions?**

 ■ **The wise men followed a star to find Jesus. How do we find him today?**

There are still a lot of things we don't know about the wise men—their names, their country or their background. But what we do know about them is wonderful. They listened to God and set aside everything else in their lives to find Jesus and worship him.

We have a different kind of journey to Jesus today. Instead of crossing the desert on camels, we have to find our way through video games, TV and all the things that make our lives busy. The baby in the manger doesn't flash on a screen or blast us with loud music. Our job is to find time to worship Jesus. You've made a good start by being here today.

Bible Verse
Glory to God in the highest, and on earth peace to men on whom his favor rests.
Luke 2:14

Lots of kids in the world today don't have the opportunity to worship. They're not allowed to learn about Jesus in the fun ways we do. They know that worshiping Jesus is a privilege. If they could be with us today, they'd think it was the coolest thing ever!

Today in your shepherd groups, you'll get to discover what worship is all about. And you won't have to cross a desert to do it! *Dismiss kids to their shepherd groups.*

2 Shepherd's Spot

Gather your small group and help kids find Matthew 2 in their Bibles.

Matthew is the very first book in the New Testament. It's the beginning of Jesus' story. Listen very carefully and see if you can catch something new in this story that you never knew before.

Have volunteers take turns reading Matthew 2:1-2 aloud. Let kids share their new thoughts about Jesus' birth.

■ **Did you ever have an important visitor at your house?**

■ **Suppose you were Mary and the wise men showed up to worship Jesus. What would you do?**

Pass out the "Starlight, Star Bright" handout. Have kids fold it in half the long way and cut out their stars. Have volunteers read the worship ideas, then brainstorm their own ideas and write them on the bottom point of the stars. Make the remaining folds to give the star dimension.

We can worship Jesus on our own, in a quiet place. We can worship Jesus with our families. And we can worship Jesus when we're together at church.

Think of the most powerful thing you've ever seen. A jet engine firing its afterburners. A huge windstorm. An earthquake. Now think about the power it took to create the world. Then imagine all that power and wisdom put into the body of a tiny baby.

Now close your eyes and think of that baby's tiny fingers wrapping around your finger. Jesus came to earth to reach out to you and show you what God is like. Let's be quiet for a moment and worship him.

After a few moments of silent worship, invite kids to share prayer concerns. Then close with prayer. **Dear Jesus, our minds can barely contain the thought of all the power of God in a tiny baby. In our hearts, we join the wise men who knelt before you. Thank you for becoming a man so you could show us what God is like. We honor you, for you are King and Lord over everything, amen.**

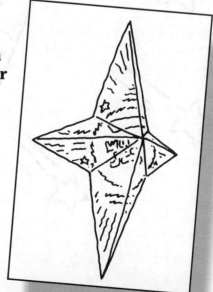

STARLIGHT, STAR BRIGHT

1. Fold the page in half the long way and line up the side points. Cut out the star.

2. Fold the star in half from side point to side point.

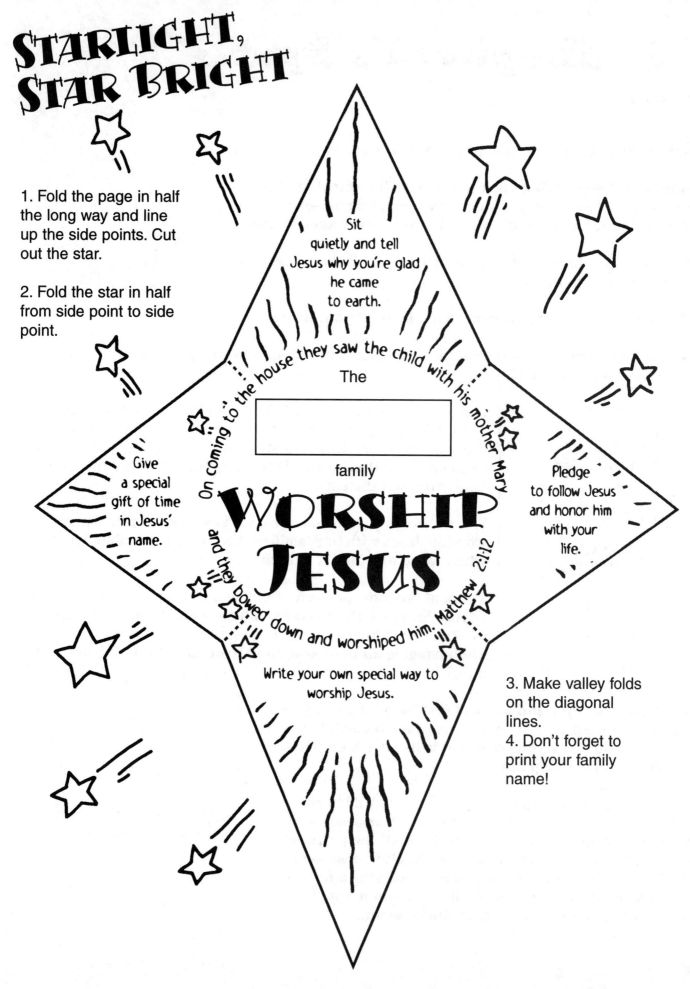

Sit quietly and tell Jesus why you're glad he came to earth.

On coming to the house they saw the child with his mother Mary

The

family

WORSHIP JESUS

and they bowed down and worshiped him. Matthew 2:11-12

Give a special gift of time in Jesus' name.

Pledge to follow Jesus and honor him with your life.

Write your own special way to worship Jesus.

3. Make valley folds on the diagonal lines.
4. Don't forget to print your family name!

Workshop Wonders

The wise men brought wonderful presents to the new baby King. Incense mentioned in today's Bible story was an expensive, sweet-smelling gummy substance that come from the branches of the Bowellia tree. Once cut, the branches oozed a whitish-yellow resin. Very smelly, but in a good way! In Bible times incense or frankincense was transported from the semi-arid mountains of Arabia, Africa and India. The wise men may have bought the precious gift from a trader traveling a long way on an ancient spice-route.

Today we'll use a sweet-smelling spice that also traveled the ancient spice route. Hold up the cinnamon sticks. **Cinnamon!** We use it today in recipes because it smells yummy and reminds us of family, home and Christmas. Let's use cinnamon to make handmade holiday ornaments to hang from our Christmas tree and remind us of the gifts the wise men gave Jesus when they worshiped him.

In a mixing bowl combine 1 cup cinnamon with 1 Tbsp. each of cloves, nutmeg and ginger. Add 1 cup of applesauce and 2 Tbsp. glue. Mix thoroughly. (For easier handling you may wish to place the dough in a refrigerator for 15 minutes.)

■ **The wise men knelt to worship baby Jesus, and then presented him with rich gifts. How will you and your family worship Jesus this Christmas?**

Dust the rolling pin and work surface with cinnamon. Roll the dough to a 1/4-inch thickness. Use cookie cutters to cut out festive Christmas shapes.

■ **What things do you first notice about a newborn baby? What do you think the wise men thought the first time they saw baby Jesus, the Savior of the world?**

Use a toothpick or drinking straw to press a hole in the ornaments. Help kids slip their ornaments onto waxed paper and into envelopes to take home. Instruct them to place the ornaments in a warm sunny spot to dry for a couple of days. Distribute lengths of red or green ribbon so kids can make hangers for their dried ornaments.

Advise your kids that even though their ornaments smell yummy, they're not for eating.

■ **Where will you hang your ornament when it's dry? What will it remind you of?**

■ **Tell a Christmas story that brings a smile to your face. How did worship play a part?**

Get List:
- ❑ bowl/rolling pin/work surface
- ❑ round cinnamon, cloves, nutmeg and ginger
- ❑ drained applesauce
- ❑ white glue
- ❑ Christmas cookie cutters
- ❑ ribbon
- ❑ toothpick or drinking straw
- ❑ Optional: waxed paper, envelopes, cinnamon sticks

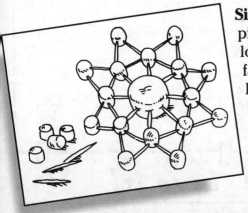

Simpler Option: Make fun Christmas snowflakes. Set out toothpicks and large and mini-marshmallows. With a large marshmallow at the center, have kids insert eight toothpicks in "daisy" fashion around the marshmallow. Let them add mini-marshmallows and more toothpicks to complete the snowflake design. For edible creations, use pretzel sticks in place of the toothpicks.

Fold down the corners to start your paper airplane.

SPECIAL DELIVERY

TO

"How do you and your family worship Jesus at Christmas? Take turns sharing details you can remember about the birth of Christ.

Today at church we learned about the birth of Jesus.

Because God sent his Son we can worship Jesus.

Collect several candles of different sizes and shapes and place them in the center of a table. Dim the lights. Gather around the table and take turns lighting the candles. Each time someone lights a candle, they finish the sentence, "Jesus, I worship you because..." When you've lit all the candles, sing "Away in a Manger" softly together. Blow out the candles. As you return the candles to their original places, think of carrying your love for Jesus to each part of the house.

Bible Verse

"Glory to God in the highest, and on earth peace to men on whom his favor rests." Luke 2:14

◊ If your family lived next door to baby Jesus, what would you bring over to celebrate his birthday?

◊ Can you name two out-of-the-ordinary ways to worship Jesus during Christmas week?

◊ What is your favorite Christmas hymn. Why?

Family FUN

Live It!

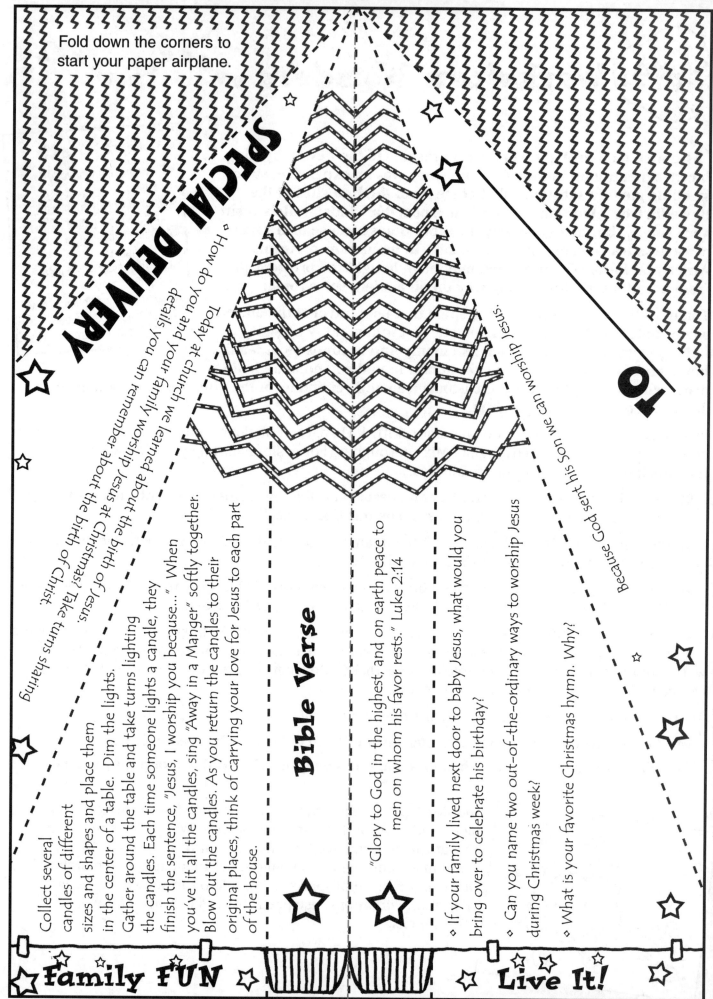

Come, Follow Me!

Get Set
LARGE GROUP ■ Greet kids and do a puppet skit. Schooner finds out the truth about Jesus' love for people.

❑ *large bird puppet* ❑ *puppeteer*

Bible 4U! Instant Drama
LARGE GROUP ■ Two vendors beside the Sea of Galilee discuss Peter and Andrew's departure to follow Jesus.

❑ *2 actors* ❑ *copies of pp. 20-21, Go Fish! script* ❑ *4 numbered balls*
Optional: ❑ *2 Bibletime costumes*

Shepherd's Spot
SMALL GROUP ■ Use the "Follow Me Folding Arrow" handout to help kids discover why they want to follow Jesus.

❑ *Bibles* ❑ *pencils* ❑ *scissors* ❑ *copies of p. 24, Follow Me Folding Arrow*
❑ *copies of p. 26, Special Delivery*

Workshop Wonders
SMALL GROUP ■ Play a lively fishing game to reinforce today's Bible verse.

❑ *badminton birdies (or paper balls)* ❑ *fishnets (or baseball gloves)*
❑ *permanent marker* ❑ *whistle*

Bible Basis Jesus calls the first disciples. Luke 5:1-11

Learn It! Jesus is our leader.

Live It! Follow Jesus!

Bible Verse I am the light of the world. Whoever follows me will never walk in darkness, but will have the light of life. John 8:12

Quick Takes

Luke 5:1-11

One day as Jesus was standing by the Lake of Gennesaret, with the people crowding round him and listening to the word of God,

2 he saw at the water's edge two boats left there by the fishermen, who were washing their nets.

3 He got into one of the boats, the one belonging to Simon, and asked him to put out a little from shore. Then he sat down and taught the people from the boat.

4 When he had finished speaking, he said to Simon, "Put out into deep water, and let down the nets for a catch."

5 Simon answered, "Master, we've worked hard all night and haven't caught anything. But because you say so, I will let down the nets."

6 When they had done so, they caught such a large number of fish that their nets began to break.

7 So they signaled to their partners in the other boat to come and help them, and they came and filled both boats so full that they began to sink.

8 When Simon Peter saw this, he fell at Jesus' knees and said, "Go away from me, Lord; I am a sinful man!"

9 For he and all his companions were astonished at the catch of fish they had taken,

10 and so were James and John, the sons of Zebedee, Simon's partners. Then Jesus said to Simon, "Don't be afraid; from now on you will catch men."

11 So they pulled their boats up on shore, left everything an followed him.

Insights

If you were going to pick twelve men to help you change the world, who would they be? Philosophers? Powerful politicians? Great public speakers? Wealthy people who could finance your cause?

Jesus chose ordinary people from the lower classes of society. His first four disciples were two pairs of brother who earned their living fishing in the Sea of Galilee. Their work was physical, tedious and tiring, not to mention smelly. You could probably "sniff out" a fisherman from several feet away!

The intellectual elite had little regard for people whose earned their living by the sweat of their brow. Common laborers didn't have time for intellectual pursuits and the serious study of Scripture.

Why would Jesus make such an unlikely choice for the first four disciples? They were humble men who would understand and have compassion for the poor. They had little reason for pride or inflated opinions of themselves. They recognized Jesus' lordship. He was different from anyone they'd ever met; his call was so compelling that it brooked no hesitation. As a result of the time they spent with Jesus, these ordinary men became world changers.

Who knows what manner of world changers you may have in your group today? Like the first disciples, the kids in your care are brimming with potential, eager to encounter a Savior who will mold their character and lead them on a life long adventure of faith. Use this lesson to challenge your kids to make a bold step of faith and answer Jesus' call.

Get Set

Get kids warmed up with some favorite songs. **Look at you guys! You know, if I had to go out and pick a bunch of kids today, I'd pick you! You're just the kind of people I like to be with. Of course, I know someone else is about to show up...***Schooner pops up.*

Schooner: Hi, boss.

Leader: Hello there, little birdie. *(Schooner and Leader sit in silence for awhile.)*

Leader: Cat got your tongue, Schooner?

Schooner: I'm thinking of taking a bath.

Leader: Now!?

Schooner: Shortly.

Leader: A bird bath, I presume.

Schooner: Squawk! I set my radar for the nearest lake and plunge right in.

Leader: Don't forget your towel.

Schooner: I'm a bird, boss. I dry as I fly.

Leader: I see. What happens if it rains?

Schooner: I take a shower!

Leader: Hmm. Well, in today's Bible story Jesus steps into a boat and heads out onto a lake.

Schooner: Bath time, huh? Don't forget the soap-on-a-rope!

Leader: No, what Jesus wants is to get a good look at the crowd who had gathered on the shore to hear him speak.

Schooner: Jesus knows a lot. He's a great teacher. So what happens next?

Leader: It's quite incredible. Amazing, really.

Schooner: *(excitedly)* What? A storm at sea?

Leader: Nope.

Schooner: Attack of the giant sea crabs?

Leader: Nope.

Schooner: Jellyfish?

Leader: Nope.

Schooner: Electric eels, a poisonous octopus, killer sharks?

Leader: Wrong again, again and again.

Schooner: I give up. What? What!

Leader: Jesus tells the fisherman near him to cast their nets into the water.

Schooner: Squawk! What's so incredible about that? Fisherman do that kind of stuff all the time.

Leader: But do they catch enough fish to fill all the plates at Lobster Shack?

Schooner: Sounds a little fishy to me.

Leader: It's written in the Bible in the book of Luke, Schooner.

Schooner: Lobster Shack is in the Bible?

Leader: No, the nets bursting full of fish.

Schooner: Ok, boss, I believe it. What happens next?

Leader: I'll give you a clue. Come follow me!

Schooner: I told you, boss. It's bath time. Really. You don't want to be around when the feathers fly.

Leader: Sure I do. I'm collecting feathers for a pillow.

Schooner: I should charge.

Leader: Not a chance. Let's go, my feathered friend. Bible 4U! is up next!

1 Bible 4U!

Hey—it's time for another edition of Bible 4U! So who's up for a visit to a lake? This is a really nice lake, great for fishing. You've probably heard of this lake before—it's called the Sea of Galilee. Jesus spent a lot of time there.

Our story happens at the time when Jesus was just beginning to attract a lot of attention. He had healed several people and crowds were starting to gather whenever he came into a town.

Instant Prep

Before class, ask two girls who are good readers to play the roles of Sheba and Rosie. Give them copies of the "Go Fish!" script below.

for Overachievers

Have a two-person drama team prepare the story. Dress them in Bible-time costumes and encourage them to be outgoing and chatty! Create a vendor's fish stand with a sign that says, "Sheba's Fish Stand." Add fishnets and wooden buckets for atmosphere.

Jesus knew it was time to get helpers—people who would be his closest friends. So he began to choose a small group of men who would travel with him wherever he went. The choices Jesus made surprised a lot of people, including the two women we're going to hear from today.

These women run a couple of food booths by the lake, so they know all about Jesus and the people who come to hear him. Listen! I hear one of them coming now.

Go Fish!
Based on Luke 5:1-11

Sheba enters.

Sheba: Welcome to Sheba's Fish Shack. We have the tastiest filets in all Capernaum, grilled fresh and served to you hot off the coals. Add a little tartar sauce and you've got yourself the best fast food in Galilee.

Talk about the perfect job! I get up in the morning; I come down to the lake, I build a little fire, clean some fish (well, I don't love that part), then I wait for all the luscious smells to bring customers to my booth. Rosemary's Bagels is right across the street. So people smell the bread baking, the fish roasting and they can't resist.

It's a good life. A little sand, a little sea, a little sun—how could it get better than that?

There's only one thing that worries me. Today I lost one of my best suppliers. You see that boat over there? It belongs to Peter and his brother Andrew. Peter's the loud-mouth—Andrew's the quiet one. They've been in the fishing business for years. And they're good. I can always count on them for a great catch. Hey…Here comes my friend Rosemary. Rosie, you got the bagels baking?

Rosie: Three batches! Business has been so good lately that I've had to double-bake.

Sheba: I know! Can you believe the crowds?

Rosie: Sure I can. It's that new rabbi, Jesus. Wherever he goes, people are sure to follow.

Sheba: You got that right.

Rosie: So did you hear about Peter and Andrew?

Sheba: Not only did I hear—I saw what happened.

Rosie: Fill me in!

Sheba: Yesterday afternoon Jesus drew the biggest crowd ever. So he got in Peter's boat and asked him to push off from the shore.

Rosie: That's smart. All the people would be able to hear him if he was a little ways out on the water.

Sheba: Exactly. Oh, does that rabbi know how to teach! He makes God sound so real—like he's right here with us.

Rosie: I know. There's something so warm about him. When he's close by, my heart seems to kind of…glow.

Sheba: I know what you mean. And Peter obviously feels that way too. When Jesus got done speaking, he told Peter to go out into deep water and let down his nets.

Rosie: You're kidding! Didn't Peter fish all night and not catch a thing?

Sheba: Yeah. And he was really tired. But he did what Jesus said, and they ended up pulling in so many fish they had to signal another boat to help. That's why I have such a big bunch to grill this morning.

Rosie: That's incredible. These "pro" fishermen can't catch anything all night, then Jesus tells them where to fish and the catch almost sinks the boat!

Sheba: Yep. Peter was pretty shook up, too. I heard that he fell on his knees before Jesus and said, "Go away from me Lord; I am a sinful man!"

Rosie: I can understand that. It's like Jesus has special powers or something.

Sheba: No doubt about it. Jesus is no ordinary man. But what happened next was even more amazing.

Rosie: Tell me! Tell me!

Sheba: Jesus said to Peter, "Don't be afraid; from now on you will catch men."

Rosie: Catch men? My cousin Esther's been trying to catch a man for years.

Sheba: No, no, Rosie. You've got it all wrong. The way Jesus said it, it meant getting other people to believe in him…to follow him.

Rosie: Oh, I get it. Well, it shouldn't be hard to get people to follow Jesus. I've never seen anyone heal people like Jesus does, or talk about God the way he does, or care about common people the way he does.

Sheba: That's what Peter thought too. Because he pulled his boat into shore and left everything behind to follow Jesus.

Rosie: Left *everything?*

Sheba: Everything. And Andrew went too.

Rosie: So that's it? No more fishing business?

Sheba: No more fishing business.

Rosie: Wow. Can you imagine leaving *everything* behind to follow Jesus?

Sheba: I don't think we've seen the last of our friends Peter and Andrew, though. Jesus seems to like visiting the towns around here.

Rosie: I'm glad. I want to hear him preach again. He's so amazing. Do you think we could… like…follow him in our hearts? I mean, believe in him?

Sheba: I'm already there, Rosie. I do believe him. I believe he shows us the way to God.

Rosie: I wish we could go with him from town to town like Peter and Andrew.

Sheba: We can keep his words with us, Rosie, and do what he teaches.

Rosie: Good thinking. Oh—I smell my bagels. And there are some customers.

Sheba: Wait a second. Take some fish from Peter's last catch.

Rosie: His last catch of *fish*, anyway. From now on he'll catch people with Jesus.

Sheba: I guess we're already caught, huh?

Rosie: By Jesus' love? You bet we are!

Peter and Andrew were the first two people Jesus asked to follow him. Then he asked another pair of brothers who were fishermen: James and John. Peter, James and John turned out to be his closest friends. Let's see how much you understand about what happened that day by the sea.

Toss the four numbered balls to different parts of the room. Bring the kids with the balls to the front one-by-one and ask these questions. Allow kids to get help from the group if they need it. After each correct answer, let kids drop the ball into a bag.

■ Why were Peter and Andrew willing to leave their business and follow Jesus?

■ You're Peter. Answer this question: "Peter, you've left the fishing business! What were you thinking?"

■ Peter did something unexpected so he could follow Jesus. What unexpected things have you done as Jesus' follower?

■ What have you "left behind" so that you can follow Jesus?

Jesus had a way of capturing people's hearts. The Jewish leaders of that time were very strict. They always talked about rules, rules, rules! When Jesus talked about the Scripture, he helped people see that God is loving and kind. And he showed that kindness in the way he healed sick people. His power amazed everyone!

Bible Verse
I am the light of the world. Whoever follows me will never walk in darkness, but will have the light of life.
John 8:12

Jesus knew he would only be on earth for a few short years. And as much as people wanted to be around him, he couldn't spend all his time with the crowds. The Bible tells us that he often went into the hills to pray. So Jesus chose twelve close friends who would be with him all the time. He could teach them everything they needed to know, then they would teach others, and those people would teach others until the Good News about Jesus spread all over the world.

The story doesn't stop with these twelve men. That's just the beginning. Jesus still calls people to follow him today—including the people in this room!

Today in your shepherd groups, you'll explore what it means to follow Jesus.

Dismiss kids to their shepherd groups.

2 Shepherd's Spot

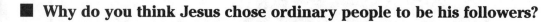

Gather your small group and help kids find Luke 5:1–11 in their Bibles.

Our Bible story today opens a new chapter in Jesus' life. He called twelve men to be his closest friends. They weren't powerful men—governors, kings or priests. He chose ordinary people like you and me. And when he said, "Follow me," they left everything and followed him. Let's read about it.

Have volunteers take turns reading Luke 5:1–11 aloud.

■ **Why do you think Jesus chose ordinary people to be his followers?**

Why were people willing to leave everything to follow Jesus? Our Bible verse gives us a clue. Distribute the "Follow Me Folding Arrow" handout and read the verse in the center together.

■ **Did you figure out the clue? Why were people willing to follow Jesus?** (So they could walk in his light.)

I wonder why you want to follow Jesus. There's a spot on one of these arrows where you can explain that. Let kids fill out the boxes in the arrows, then fold and cut the handout to make an arrow booklet. Invite kids to share as they write.

Your arrow booklets point you forward on the path of following Jesus. It's an exciting adventure—more exciting than you could ever imagine! It's an adventure we're on together, with Jesus as our leader. We're here each week to learn from Jesus and encourage each other. Let's encourage each other right now by praying for things that are important to each of us.

Encourage kids to share their prayer requests. Then close with a prayer similar to this one. **Dear Jesus, it's incredible to learn about the amazing things you did and the way you cared for people. We know that you care about us too, so today we're praying for these special things.** (Mention each child's request.) **We're excited about following you and we ask you to help us do that this week. In your name we pray, amen.**

FOLLOW ME FOLDING ARROW

1. Cut out the square.
2. Fold each way in half on the dotted lines.
3. Cut out the arrow shape.
4. Complete the sentences on each arrow.

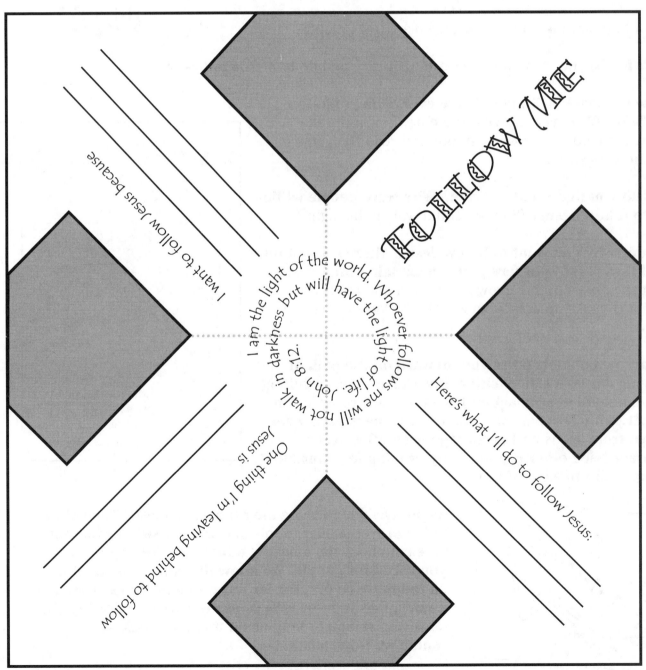

I want to follow Jesus because

Here's what I'll do to follow Jesus:

One thing I'm leaving behind to follow Jesus is

I am the light of the world. Whoever follows me will not walk in darkness but will have the light of life. John 8:12.

FOLLOW ME

Workshop Wonders

The fisherman in today's story were pretty sure that this day would be like any other. *Let's see. We need to clean the nets, mend the nets, weight the nets and then cast the nets into the sea—and hope for the biggest catch of fish ever!* Unfortunately for our fisherman, hope—in the way of fish—did not rise to the surface. Simon Peter may have thought he knew more about fishing than Jesus, but he "followed the leader" and obeyed Jesus' command. And in no time at all a large catch of fish was his reward. Peter and his fishing buddies followed the leader's call to leave their past behind and give their future to Jesus.

Get List:
- ❑ badminton birdies or paper balls
- ❑ fishnets or baseball mitts
- ❑ whistle
- ❑ permanent marker

Let's play a catch and release game of our own!

Form groups of six or larger. **I'll need a volunteer from each group to be a "net" to net the chance to catch a fish!** Hand each volunteer a fish net.

If you don't have fish nets and badminton birdies, substitute catchers' mitts and balls of wadded paper. Ask the remaining kids to grab chairs and form sitting circles around the volunteers.

As kids arrange themselves, use the marker to draw a fish face on the rubber end of each badminton birdie. Hold the badminton "fishes" up for your class to see. Then hand one off to each group.

On my count, begin tossing your "fish" to someone opposite you in the circle. But beware! The "net" in the middle will try and catch it. If the "net" catches the fish, the last player to touch it must say today's Bible verse before giving up his or her seat to become the new "net." No wild throws, please. Ready? One...two...three. Go fish!

If you want to pump up the volume, play music with a lively beat as kids play. After a couple of minutes blow your whistle to stop play and have kids scramble into new groups.

Collect the nets and birdies and have kids gather in a large group. Have everyone take a few deep breaths to cool down.

The fisherman in today's story left everything to follow Jesus. Let's all be willing to leave behind the things we treasure most to follow the Savior of the world.

- ■ **How would you go about "catching" someone for Jesus? What would you do? What would you say?**
- ■ **Can you think of someone you could "catch" for Jesus?**

Fold down the corners to start your paper airplane.

SPECIAL DELIVERY

TO

Today at church we learned how Jesus called disciples to follow him.
"Jesus performed a miracle in today's story. Who saw the miracle?
What did they do?"

Jesus is our leader. Follow Jesus!

Family FUN

Jesus told the fishermen in today's story, "Follow me." See if you can follow your ears into some Bible fun with your family. Put a handful of fish crackers into a plastic container. Have the other players give you one minute to find the perfect hiding place. Once you're hidden, give the box of crackers a shake every few seconds. See how quickly your family members can follow the sound to find you. When you've been found, answer one of the following questions together. Let others take turns hiding until you've answered all the questions.

Bible Verse

"I am the light of the world. Whoever follows me will never walk in darkness, but will have the light of life."
John 8:12

Live It!

If your family lived next to a beach, what washed-up items could you collect that would remind you of today's Bible story?

◊ How do people get "caught" by Jesus' love?

◊ What do you think children standing on the shore in today's Bible story thought of the catch of fish the fishermen brought to shore?

The Wedding at Cana

Get Set
LARGE GROUP ■ Greet kids and do a puppet skit. Schooner reveals his misunderstanding of weddings.

❏ large bird puppet ❏ puppeteer

Bible 4U! Instant Drama
LARGE GROUP ■ Jars 1, 2 and 3 tell the story of Jesus' miracle at the wedding.

❏ 3 actors ❏ signs or cardboard jars numbered 1, 2, 3
❏ copies of pp. 30-31, A Jarring Experience ❏ 4 numbered balls

Shepherd's Spot
SMALL GROUP ■ Use the "Jars of Faith" handout to encourage kids to trust Jesus with their problems. Share concerns and pray together. Send home the Special Delivery handout.

❏ Bibles ❏ pencils ❏ scissors ❏ copies of p. 34, Jars of Faith ❏ copies of p. 36, Special Delivery

Workshop Wonders
SMALL GROUP ■ Build small clay jars and tuck notes of faith inside.

❏ super dough or self-hardening clay ❏ waxed paper ❏ permanent marker
Optional: ❏ small plastic jewels ❏ tiny shells ❏ toothpick ❏ scissors
❏ construction paper

Bible Basis
John 2:1-11
Jesus does his first miracle.

Learn It!
There's no problem Jesus can't solve.

Live It!
Trust Jesus with all your problems.

Bible Verse
Do not let your hearts be troubled. Trust in God; trust also in me.
John 14:1

Quick Takes

John 2:1-11

On the third day a wedding took place at Cana in Galilee. Jesus' mother was there,
2 and Jesus and his disciples had also been invited to the wedding.
3 When the wine was gone, Jesus' mother said to him, "They have no more wine."
4 "Dear woman, why do you involve me?" Jesus replied. "My time has not yet come."
5 His mother said to the servants, "Do whatever he tells you."
6 Nearby stood six stone water jars, the kind used by the Jews for ceremonial washing, each holding from twenty to thirty gallons.
7 Jesus said to the servants, "Fill the jars with water;" so they filled them to the brim.
8 Then he told them, "Now draw some out and take it to the master of the banquet." They did so,
9 and the master of the banquet tasted the water that had been turned into wine. He did not realize where it had come from, though the servants who had drawn the water knew. Then he called the bridegroom aside
10 and said, "Everyone brings out the choice wine first and then the cheaper wine after the guests have had too much to drink; but you have saved the best till now."
11 This, the first of his miraculous signs, Jesus performed at Cana in Galilee. He thus revealed his glory, and his disciples put their faith in him.

Insights

Jesus lived quietly with his family until his early thirties. When the time was right, he went to John to be baptized. After 40 days of temptation in the wilderness, Jesus began his ministry in earnest by calling disciples who would travel with him and carry his message. These men willingly left families and occupations behind to follow an amazing young rabbi who was just beginning to make a name for himself. What would their lives be like? What were they getting into? They were about to find out!

All five attended a wedding in Cana. Jesus' mother was also there. The wedding host must have miscalculated the amount of wine he would need to accommodate the crowd, for not long into the celebration, Jesus' mother came to him saying, "They have no more wine." Though Jesus was reluctant to draw attention to himself, Mary had no doubt that her son could solve the problem. At his command, servants filled six jars with water. But the liquid they poured from the jars moments later was fine wine.

According to John, Jesus had a larger motive that just saving a wedding banquet from ruin. The miracle confirmed his followers' faith and gave a public demonstration that he was no ordinary itinerant rabbi.

In our complicated, sometimes terrifying world, kids need faith builders. They need to know that Jesus is not above caring about their everyday problems. Use this lesson to introduce them to the Savior who is more than able to inspire faith and work miraculously in their lives.

Option Get Set

Hey, it's nice to see all your smiling faces. I'm glad you're here today because there's no better place to be than God's house. We're here for a reason—to learn about Jesus and how much he loves us! And I have a friend here who's going to help us. *Schooner pops up.*

Schooner: Hi, boss!

Leader: Hey there, Schooner.

Schooner: Guess where I got to go yesterday.

Leader: Where?

Schooner: To a wedding. I love weddings. Especially the cake part. Big white fluffy mounds of frosting that gets all over your beak. Mmm! Mmm! Mmm!

Leader: What else makes weddings so special.

Schooner: Punch! Peanuts! And all those buttery little mints.

Leader: I think you're missing the point, Schooner.

Schooner: What point? Where? Um, would you lean toward me for just a sec?

Leader leans toward Schooner. Schooner examines the top of his head.

Schooner: Oh, that point! *(cracks himself up)*

Leader: *(slightly scolding)* Schooner…

Schooner: Sorry, boss.

Leader: The point of a wedding is that a man and a woman are joining themselves together with a lifelong pledge of love.

Schooner: Eeeeu-YUCK!

Leader: *(slightly scolding)* Schooner…

Schooner: I think you got it wrong boss. It's about the food. Everybody knows weddings are about the food. *(to kids)* What do you guys think? Is it about *(mocking)* "love, sweet love," or it about the food? *(pauses)* FOOD! FOOD!

Leader: Schooner, cut it out already!

Schooner: It worries me when you have your priorities so messed up, boss. I mean, there are a lot of us out there who go to weddings for the cake and punch and peanuts. And, oh man, when they throw the birdseed on the bride and groom at the end. Mmm-mmm! What a feast!

Leader: Okay, Schooner, I get the point. You know, you would have loved going to weddings in Bible times.

Schooner: Oh yeah. Why?

Leader: For the food. They held a huge feast that went on for hours and hours. Sometimes even days!

Schooner: Woohoo! That's what I'm talkin' about. I am SO there, baby. So, boss, what kind of food did they serve?

Leader: Figs, grapes, bread, wine, roasted parrot…

Schooner: *(hides behind leader as he yells)* Ahhh!

Leader: Hey, come out of there, Schooner. I was only teasing.

Schooner: *(comes out resentfully)* It wasn't funny.

Leader: I owed you one.

Schooner: Humph!

Leader: I know a Bible story about a wedding feast.

Schooner: Really?

Leader: Yup. You wanna hear about it?

Schooner: Is there gonna be food?

Leader: No, but there's gonna be a miracle.

Schooner: What's a miracle?

Leader: When you're nice to me.

Schooner: Hey!

Leader: A miracle is something that only God can do.

Schooner: Cool. I'm ready.

Leader: Okay—here's the Bible 4U!

1 Bible 4U!

Have the "jars" stand facing away from the audience until you cue them to turn around.

Welcome to today's edition of Bible 4U Theater. Today we find ourselves at a wedding in the small town of Cana, just a few miles west of the Sea of Galilee. There's a celebrity coming to this wedding— an up and coming rabbi who grew up just south of here in the town of Nazareth. This rabbi, Jesus, has begun to gather a group of followers. Nobody important—just some fishermen, a couple of pairs of brothers, a few other people he's met here and there. It's a strange thing with these followers of Jesus. They just picked up and left their jobs to follow him. You know—"Hey, everybody, I'm going with Jesus now. 'Bye! Don't leave the light on for me." Then they hit the road and followed Jesus.

Jesus and his followers will be guests at today's wedding. Folks are kind of curious about them. Jesus' mother will be there too. We don't have an invitation, so let's just slip in by these big jars. Come with me—quietly—and try to blend in with the crowd.

Instant Prep

Make three construction paper signs for actor to wear, labeled Jar 1, Jar 2 and Jar 3. Before class, ask three volunteers who are good readers to play the roles of the jars in the Bible story. Give them copies of the "Jarring Experience" script below.

for Overachievers

Make 3 large (person-sized) cardboard jar shapes similar to the jars on p. 34. Label them Jar 1, Jar 2 and Jar 3 and attach a string actors can loop around their shoulders. Have a three person drama team prepare the Bible story.

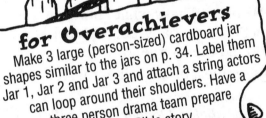

A Jarring Experience
Based on John 2:1–11

Jar 1: *(wailing)* Waaaaa! Boo-hoo-hoo-hoo!

Jar 2: Hey! Whattsa matter?

Jar 1: I always cry at weddings.

Jar 3: Why?

Jar 1: Because the bride is just so *(sob!)* bee-yootiful.

Jar 2: How corny is that? You're crying because the bride is beautiful. Puh-leeze.

Jar 3: Yeah, well the truth is we've got more important things to cry about.

Jar 1: What's that?

Jar 3: Something really embarrassing is about to happen.

Jar 1: Why—does somebody have indigestion? *(snorts with laughter)*

Jar 3: No, silly. Have you noticed sort of an empty feeling?

Jar 2: *(gasps)* Oh, no! We're almost empty!

Jar 3: We're runnin' on fumes, baby.

Jar 1: All these wedding guests—they won't have a thing to drink! And it's a hot day!

Jar 2: And the host will be embarrassed!

Jar 3: And the wedding will be ruined!

ALL: Waaa!

Jar 2: Wait—see that lady over there? She's noticed our problem.

Jar 3: I know who she is. She's Mary—from Nazareth. Have you heard all the talk about her son, Jesus?

Jar 1: Yeah—he's starting to form a group of followers. Some fishermen and a couple of other guys.

Jar 2: Right! People are expecting great things from him. I don't know what kinds of great things exactly, but…

Jar 3: Shhh! I think we're about to find out!

Jar 1: I can't hear. Tell me what's goin' on!

Jar 2: Mary told Jesus that the wine is almost gone. Then she told the servants to do whatever he tells them. And he told them…

ALL: Who-o-o-o-a!

Jar 2:: …to fill us up with water.

Jar 1: Water! But they can't serve water to the guests.

Jar 3: Oooh—*(giggles)* that water's cold!

Jar 1: No kiddin! Feels kind of good, if you ask me.

Jar 2: Here comes a servant with a dipper. Button it up!

All three jars freeze.

Jar 3: The coast is clear. He's gone. And he's taking a sip to the master of the feast.

Jar 1: But it was just water…

Jar 2: Was being the operative word. Take a whiff. What do you smell?

Jar 3: W-w-w-w-wine! Really good wine! The best wine I've ever held!

Jar 1: How did that happen?

Jar 2: He did it. Jesus. He changed the water into wine.

Jar 3: Are you thinkin' what I'm thinkin'?

Jar 2: What—that this is a miracle? Yep, that's exactly what I'm thinkin'.

Jar 1: And we were part of it. Oh, this is so exciting!

Jar 3: Hold on there. Don't get excited. You know what happens when you get excited.

Jar 1: Don't worry. I'll contain myself.

Jar 2: Listen! The wedding guests are talking about how good the wine is. And how strange it is that the host saved the best wine until now.

Jar 3: Well, it's not like anybody knew Jesus was going to do this miracle. Do you see how his followers are looking at him?

Jar 1: Mmm-hmm. Like he's a god or something.

Jar 2: Here's what I'm thinkin'. We've been standing in this corner for quite a few years now. And we've heard a lot of people talking about waiting for the Messiah to come— someone who would bring peace and lead the people to God. Do you suppose this Jesus could be the one?

Jar 3: That's exactly what I was thinking.

Jar 1: It all makes sense. If you ask my opinion, I think Jesus did this miracle today to help people believe in him.

Jar 2: Right! Some folks have already figured out the fact that he's a great teacher. But now they'll realize he's a lot more than that.

Jar 3: It was pretty nice of him to take care of our little problem here today. I mean, he's not like some of those teachers who just like to hear themselves talk. Jesus cares about people's problems.

Jar 2: So now nobody has anything to "wine" about.

Jar 1: Yeah, if Jesus hadn't been here, this would have been a jarring experience.

Jar 2: But Jesus made it quite ful-filling.

Jar 3: Oh, man. You guys are really pouring it on. I'd be grape-ful if you'd stop making puns.

Jar 1: Hey—we're just claying around.

Jar 3: Well try putting a lid on it.

Jar 1: I can't—my mouth is too big. Wait a minute—I didn't say that. I-did-not-say-that!

Jar 2: I didn't hear a thing. I'm stone deaf.

Jar 1: Oh, stop. You're crackin' me up. And then I'll be out of a job.

Jar 3: Shh! Here comes a servant for a refill.

Jar 2: I remember him—the big dipper! Ha!

Jars 1 and 2: Shh!

Jars freeze.

Bible 4U!

Let's have a big hand for the three jars! Now I have some questions to toss out. Toss the four numbered balls to different parts of the room.

Let's see if we can bag some answers. Who has ball #1?

Bring the kids with the balls to the front one-by-one and ask these questions. Allow kids to get help from the group if they need it. After each correct answer, let kids drop the ball into a bag.

 ■ **What was the big problem in this story?**

 ■ **How did Jesus solve it?**

 ■ **Why did Jesus do that?**

 ■ **Suppose you were a guest at the wedding. What would you tell your neighbor about Jesus?**

If you wish, toss out small wrapped candies when all the balls are in the bag.

Good thinking! The Bible tells us that Jesus did this miracle so his disciples would put their faith in him. Our story happened at the beginning of Jesus' ministry. He was about 30 years old, and had just begun to let people know that he was more than a carpenter's son.

Bible Verse
Do not let your hearts be troubled. Trust in God; trust also in me.
John 14:1

Over the next two-and-a-half years, Jesus taught, healed people, calmed storms and fed great crowds. He showed us that he cares for us and that there isn't a single problem in the whole world he can't solve. That's pretty exciting news— news that's just as important to us today as it was back in Bible times. Today in your small groups you'll learn what it really means to trust in Jesus.

 *Dismiss the kids to their small groups.*

2 Shepherd's Spot

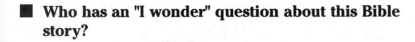

Gather your small group and help kids find John 2 in their Bibles.

■ **Who can name the first four books of the New Testament?**

Matthew, Mark, Luke and John are called the gospels. Gospel means Good News! These good news books tell us about the life of Jesus. Each book gives us a slightly different point of view. John was from the other three.

Have volunteers takes turns reading John 2:1-11 aloud.

■ **Who has an "I wonder" question about this Bible story?**

Encourage kids to discuss their questions and thoughts. Then pass out the "Jars of Faith" handout. Show kids how to fold the page in half the long way, cut out the jar shapes and fold them into a booklet.

Give kids ample time to complete each page of the booklet. Pair readers with non-readers, or work through the booklet together. Allow volunteers to tell how they completed each page.

It's great to be able to trust Jesus with all our problems, big or small, and know that he cares. I'd like to pray about some of the things you just shared. Is there anything else you'd like me to pray about this week?

Listen carefully to kids' concerns, then close with a prayer similar to this one.

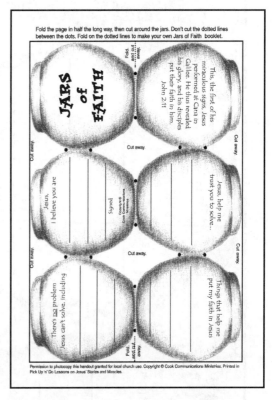

Fold the page in half the long way, then cut around the jars. Don't cut the dotted lines between the dots. Fold on the dotted lines to make your own Jars of Faith booklet.

JARS of FAITH

This, the first of his miraculous signs, Jesus performed at Cana in Galilee. He thus revealed his glory, and his disciples put their faith in him. John 2:11

Jesus, I believe you are

Signed

Jesus, help me trust you to solve...

There's no problem Jesus can't solve, including

Things that help me put my faith in Jesus

JARS of FAITH

Dear Jesus, thank you for all the ways you showed us that we can trust in you. Thank you for caring about the problems that come up in our lives. I pray for (mention each child by name, along with the concerns kids mentioned). Help us remember to trust in you, amen.

Fold the page in half the long way, then cut around the jars.
Don't cut the dotted lines between the dots.
Fold on the dotted lines to make your own Jars of Faith booklet.

Fold and cut away.

Cut away.

Cut away.

JARS of FAITH

This, the first of his miraculous signs, Jesus performed at Cana in Galilee. He thus revealed his glory, and his disciples put their faith in him. John 2:11

Jesus, I believe you are

Signed

Copyright © Cook Communications Ministries

Jesus, help me trust you to solve...

There's no problem Jesus can't solve, including

Things that help me put my faith in Jesus

Fold and cut away.

Option Workshop Wonders

What a surprise at the wedding! The hosts were panicked when they realized they didn't have enough for the thirsty guests to drink. Jesus told the servants to fill the jars with water, but what came out of the jars was wine. Jesus showed everyone that there's no problem he can't solve. Let's make our own clay jars to remember Jesus' first miracle.

Get List:
- ❑ super dough or self-hardening clay
- ❑ waxed paper
- ❑ permanent marker

Optional
- ❑ plastic jewels
- ❑ tiny shells
- ❑ toothpick
- ❑ construction paper
- ❑ scissors

Write children's' names in permanent marker on waxed paper squares. Distribute the squares. Then hand each child a two-inch ball of clay. Suggest that they try one of these ways to build their clay jars.

Demonstrate how to separate the clay into three smaller pliable balls. Gently roll each ball with an open palm to create three "snakes" of clay about the same width and length. Coil one length of clay into a flat circle. This will be the base of the jar. Wrap the two remaining clay ropes around the base, working upward, to form the sides of the jar. Tell kids to gently press the clay coils together as they work.

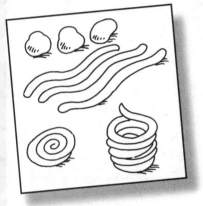

A simpler method is to have the kids knead their clay into a pliable "egg." Show them how to mold the dough around an index finger, making sure to leave plenty of dough at the tip to form a sturdy base for the jar. To make the base, press a finger against the waxed paper and smooth the dough down to broaden it. Then work the dough upward to form the body of the jar. Kids can gently remove their fingers from the jar and trim the opening with scissors.

Decorating the jar is half the fun! Kids can press shells or jewels into the clay, or incise simple designs with a toothpick.

Make faith slips from construction paper strips. Have kids write or draw problems they can trust Jesus to solve. Place the rolled slips in the jars, along with a few "blanks" to be filled in later. Tell kids to carry their jars carefully and allow a day for them to dry fully.

As kids work, talk about:

■ How did Jesus make "something" from "nothing special"?

■ What do you think the bride and groom said to Jesus when word of his miracle got around?

■ When did Jesus take care of a big problem for you?

When you show your jar to your family, tell them the story about Jesus' miracle and invite them to write faith slips of their own to add to the jar!

Fold down the corners to start your paper airplane.

SPECIAL DELIVERY

TO

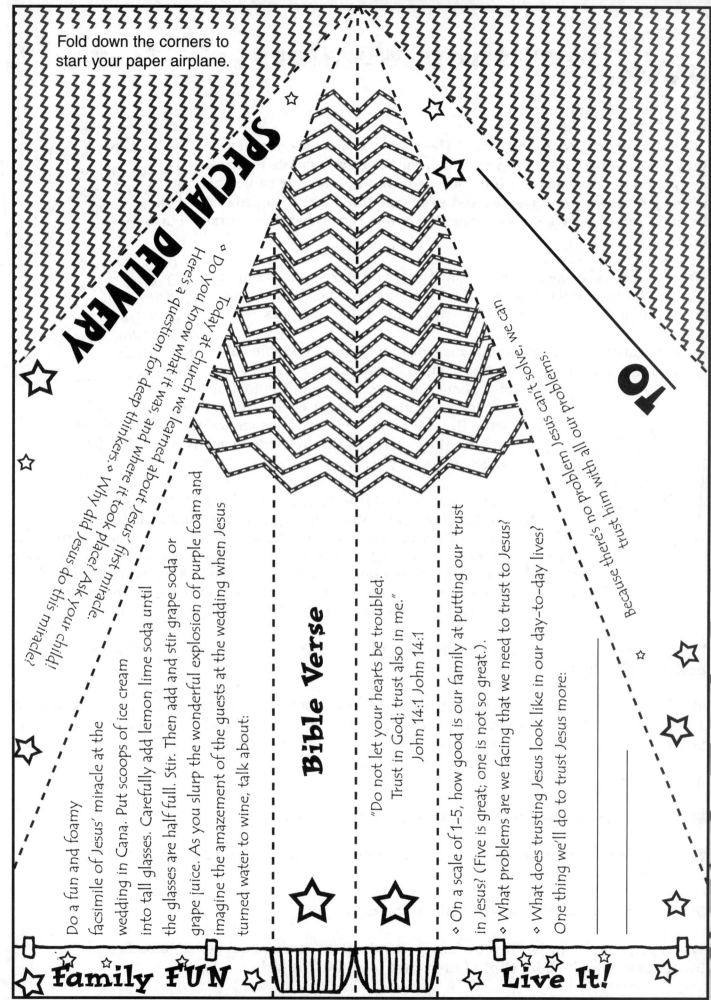

Do you know what it was?

Today at church we learned about Jesus' first miracle. Here's a question for deep thinkers: Why did Jesus do this miracle? Ask your child!

Do a fun and foamy facsimile of Jesus' miracle at the wedding in Cana. Put scoops of ice cream into tall glasses. Carefully add lemon lime soda until the glasses are half full. Stir. Then add and stir grape soda or grape juice. As you slurp the wonderful explosion of purple foam and imagine the amazement of the guests at the wedding when Jesus turned water to wine, talk about:

Bible Verse

"Do not let your hearts be troubled. Trust in God; trust also in me."
John 14:1 John 14:1

◇ On a scale of 1-5, how good is our family at putting our trust in Jesus? (Five is great; one is not so great.).
◇ What problems are we facing that we need to trust to Jesus?
◇ What does trusting Jesus look like in our day-to-day lives?
◇ One thing we'll do to trust Jesus more:

_____

Because there's no problem Jesus can't solve, we can trust him with all our problems.

Family FUN

Live It!

Lessons on a Hillside

Option

Get Set
LARGE GROUP ■ Greet kids and do a puppet skit. Schooner learns to be a light for Jesus.

❑ large bird puppet ❑ puppeteer

1

Bible 4U! Instant Drama
LARGE GROUP ■ Four contemporary vignettes illustrate the challenge of living the way Jesus teaches us to live.

❑ 5 actors ❑ copies of pp. 40-41, Words to Live By script ❑ 4 numbered balls Optional: ❑ pizza box

2

Shepherd's Spot
SMALL GROUP ■ Use the "Words to Live By" handout to help kids explore ways to live out Jesus' teaching.

❑ Bibles ❑ pencils ❑ scissors ❑ copies of p. 44, Words to Live By ❑ copies of p. 46, Special Delivery

Option

Workshop Wonders
SMALL GROUP ■ A salt-water experiment illustrates the "light" of today's Bible verse.

❑ cups ❑ vegetable oil ❑ salt ❑ water ❑ measuring cups

Bible Basis
Sermon on the Mount—Matthew 5:13–16, 43–45; 6:25–26, 33; 7:24–29

Learn It!
Jesus teaches us how to live.

Live It!
Let your light shine!

Bible Verse
"Let your light shine before men, that they may see your good deeds and praise your Father in heaven." Matthew 5:16

Quick Takes

You are the salt of the earth...You are the light of the world. A city on a hill cannot be hidden. Neither do people light a lamp and put it under a bowl. Instead they put it on its stand, and it gives light to everyone in the house. In the same way, let your light shine before men, that they may see your good deeds and praise your Father in heaven." (5:13-16)

"You have heard that it was said, 'Love your neighbor and hate your enemy.' But I tell you: Love your enemies and pray for those who persecute you, that you may be sons of your Father in heaven. He causes his sun to rise on the evil and the good, and sends rain on the righteous and the unrighteous." (5:43-45)

"Therefore I tell you, do not worry about your life, what you will eat or drink; or about your body, what you will wear. Is not life more important than food, and the body more important than clothes? Look at the birds of the air; they do not sow or reap or store away in barns, and yet your heavenly Father feeds them. Are you not much more valuable than they? But seek first his kingdom and his righteousness, and all these things will be given to you as well." (6:25–26, 33)

"Therefore everyone who hears these words of mine and puts them into practice is like a wise man who built his house on the rock. The rain came down, the streams rose, and the winds blew and beat against that house; yet it did not fall, because it had its foundation on the rock. But everyone who hears these words of mine and does not put them into practice is like a foolish man who built his house on sand. The rain came down, the streams rose, and the winds blew and beat against that house, and it fell with a great crash." When Jesus had finished saying these things, the crowds were amazed at his teaching, because he taught as one who had authority, and not as their teachers of the law. (7:24-29)

Insights

Jesus knew how to drop a gauntlet! When people gathered on a mountainside to listen, they didn't go away disappointed. Jesus took the traditional legalistic view of life as taught by the scribes and turned it on its ear. How radical was his teaching?

Retribution and payback had been a part of the Jewish system since Moses' time. Instead of "an eye for an eye," Jesus said, "Love your enemies." Self-righteous Pharisees made a great public show of fasting and praying. Jesus said, "When you pray, go into your room, close the door and pray."

Any respectable Jew would avoid sinners, and they scrutinized each other's religious practices with a spirit of one-upmanship. Jesus said: "Do not judge or you too will be judged."

Besides setting a new standard for attitudes, Jesus addressed the most heartfelt needs of his listeners. He said to pray for daily needs instead of worrying about them. He assured them that God is aware of and attentive to their needs. What a different picture of God Jesus painted!

In the Sermon on the Mount, Jesus set the bar high. Impossibly high from a human perspective. How can kids—or adults—begin to live out the lessons Jesus taught here? By committing ourselves to "your will be done" (6:10). By acknowledging that our loving God already knows our needs and surrounds us with his loving care.

These teachings of Jesus are as radical and counter-cultural for kids today as they were in Jesus' time. Love your enemies? Forget it. Payback is sweet—go for it. And who doesn't worry about clothes and looking cool? Who doesn't worry, period? Use this lesson to help kids understand that when Jesus asks these things of us, he also gives us his presence and power to live up to them.

Option: Get Set

Welcome! I'm glad to have your company this morning and to share the light of God's love with each of you. I have a friend who is always available to help me out. Are you there, Schooner? *Schooner pops up.*

Schooner: Bright eyed and bushy-tailed!

Leader: There you are! I'm glad you're here, Schooner.

Schooner: Me too.

Leader: So do you have plans for the day?

Schooner: I don't like plants, boss. I always forget to water 'em.

Leader: Not *plants*, Schooner. Plans.

Schooner: Plans?

Leader: *(scratches head)* Hmm. Let's say today is a shopping day. You make a menu for the week, check the fridge, make a list, clip a few coupons, check the ads in the newspaper and head for the grocery store.

Schooner: Grocery store?

Leader: A place to buy pickles, carrots, salt...berries...

Schooner: Berries...oh, you mean food!

Leader: *(looks out towards the group)* I think he's got it!

Schooner: I don't make plans to go food shopping, boss.

Leader: Not ever?

Schooner: No-no, never-never, uh-uh-uh!

Leader: But you love to eat!

Schooner: Yep. Eating's my favorite pastime.

Leader: Well then...

Schooner: Think about it, boss. I'm not a frozen dinner kind of guy.

Leader: Oh, I get it!

Schooner: It's about time. Everything I need...

Leader: ...comes straight from the hand of God.

Schooner: That's right. Everyday is an all-you-can-eat buffet. Seeds, berries, the occasional fresh little fish. God provides everything that I need every day!

Leader: That's awe-some.

Schooner: Yes, siree! No check cards. No lines. It's food for the picking!

Leader: God takes care of all of us. He loves us that much. But he also wants us to obey his Word and do what's right.

Schooner: *(smugly)* I'm a pretty good egg if I do say so myself.

Leader: Pretty good doesn't hold much salt with Jesus, Schooner.

Schooner: Huh?

Leader: How Jesus sees us is what's important. Did you know that Jesus wants us to be salty for him? Like a sprinkle of salt on a French fry!

Schooner: I wanna be a French fry for Jesus!

Leader: You don't need to be a French fry!

Schooner: But you just said...*squawk!*

Leader: What I mean to say, Schooner, is that we need to live like Jesus. Have his love burn bright in our hearts...

Schooner: I can do that!

Leader: ... so people can see Jesus in us...

Schooner: I can do that!

Leader: ...and to love others who don't like us and treat us badly.

Schooner: *(shakes head) Squawk!* I can't do that.

Leader: It's hard. But with God's help you can do it and do it well.

Schooner: But I'm just a little bird.

Leader: I'll help you, Schooner.

Schooner: Promise?

Leader: God promises. Let's trust in him.

Leader & Schooner: *(hugs all around)* Bible 4U! up next!

1 Bible 4U!

Welcome to Bible 4U! Theater. It's another lovely day by the Sea of Galilee.

Do you feel that cool breeze off the lake? Don't you love the sounds of the waves lapping the shore? Jesus has headed up a mountainside near here to teach the crowds of people who have gathered. They don't know it yet, but Jesus is about to turn their world upside down.

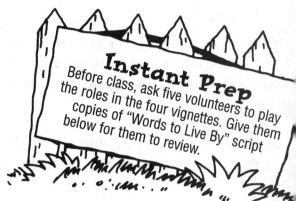

Instant Prep
Before class, ask five volunteers to play the roles in the four vignettes. Give them copies of "Words to Live By" script below for them to review.

for Overachievers
Have a five-person drama team prepare the story. Dress the Pizza Person in a cap and apron and give him or her an empty pizza box. Place copies of the Scripture passages in the box.

You see, before Jesus came, God's people tried to live by a set of rules God gave to Moses. They called it "The Law." They thought if you live by the Law and do all the right things, you're good. The strict laws made sure God's people lived in peace with God and with each other. It made sure people treated each other fairly.

But Jesus took the ideas of the Law beyond how we act. He taught that how we think is important, too. Today you'll hear his words in between scenes of our drama. Listen carefully. Do you think you'd be able to live up to what he asks?

Words to Live By
Based on Matthew 5:13–16, 43–45; 6:25–26, 31; 7:24–29

Scene 1

Kid 1: Hey—I got some eggs from the fridge. And I have plans.

Kid 2: Oh yeah?

Kid 1: You know that mean guy up the street who yells at us?

Kid 2: Uh-huh.

Kid 1: He's got a nice, shiny new car. I think it would look better with a few smashed eggs.

Kid 2: Sounds fun.

Kid 1: Let's do it after dark.

Kid 2: I'm in.

Pizza Person: *(interrupting)* Delivery! (Reads Matthew 5:13-16) Replay! *(exits)*

Kid 1: Hey—I got some eggs from the fridge. And I have plans.

Kid 2: Oh yeah?

Kid 1: You know that mean guy up the street who yells at us?

Kid 2: Uh-huh.

Kid 1: He's got a nice, shiny new car. I think it would look better with a few smashed eggs.

Kid 2: Bad idea.

Kid 1: Why not?

Kid 2: He probably likes his eggs scrambled, with nice crispy bacon.

Kid 1: Oh, man—you're no fun at all.

Kid 2: We could crack the eggs over your head. Mom says protein is good for your hair.

Kid 1: Yuck!

Scene 2

Kid 1: Do you see what I see?

Kid 2: Yep. That girl who said we were cheating is heading our way with a pile of art supplies so high she can't see over it.

Kid 1: We weren't cheating.

Kid 2: We never cheat.

Kid 1: We could trip her and she'd fall on her face.

Kid 2: And her stuff would go all over the hall.

Kid 1: And she'd be totally humiliated.

Kid 2: And we would laugh for three hours.

Kid 1: Schweet!

Pizza Person: *(interrupting)* Delivery! (Reads Matthew 5:43-45) Replay! *(exits)*

Kid 1: Do you see what I see?

Kid 2: Yep. That girl who said we were cheating is heading our way with a pile of art supplies so high she can't see over it.

Kid 1: We weren't cheating.

Kid 2: We never cheat.

Kid 1: We could trip her and she'd fall flat on her face.

Kid 2: And her stuff would go all over the hall.

Kid 1: And she'd be totally humiliated.

Kid 2: And then we'd feel bad about it.

Kid 1: Because we'd be treating her like she treated us.

Kid 2: We'd be dirty rotten creeps. I have another idea. Let's help her carry the stuff.

Kid 1: Yeah! That would shock her socks off.

Kid 2: So let's go turn an enemy into a friend.

Scene 3

Daughter: We're taking school pictures today and I haven't got anything to wear!

Mom: We bought clothes last weekend. How about your blue top?

Daughter: No way.

Mom: Your purple sweater.

Daughter: I'd look like a complete dork.

Mom: Your jean vest.

Daughter: We've gotta go to the mall.

Mom: I just spent a hundred dollars on clothes!

Daughter: Fine. I'll just look like a loser.

Pizza Person: *(interrupting)* Delivery! (Reads Matthew 6:25-26, 31) Replay! *(exits)*

Daughter: We're taking school pictures today and I haven't got anything to wear!

Mom: We bought clothes last weekend. How about your blue top?

Daughter: No way.

Mom: Your purple sweater.

Daughter: I'd look like a complete dork.

Mom: Your jean vest.

Daughter: That's so old. We've gotta go to the mall.

Mom: I just spent a hundred dollars on clothes.

Daughter: What would I look good in?

Mom: I know.

Daughter: What?

Mom: Your smile!

Daughter: You mean this one? *(sticks fingers in the sides of her mouth and stretches her grin)*

Mom: That one! Nobody will even notice what you're wearing.

Daughter: It's a plan! You know, people say I look just like you.

Mom: *(stretches her grin)* I wonder why they say that!

Scene 4

Kid 1: You know all this stuff we've been hearing at church?

Kid 2: That love your enemies, let your light shine stuff?

Kid 1: Yeah. It's hard.

Kid 2: And it's not fun either.

Kid 1: You need to get in a little trouble every day to keep things interesting.

Kid 1: Pick on new kids, bully people...

Kid 2: Mouth off at your parents...

Kid 1: Get back at anybody who messes with you.

Pizza Person: *(interrupting)* Delivery! (Reads Matthew 7:24-29) Replay! *(exits)*

Kid 1: You know all this stuff we've been hearing at church?

Kid 2: That love your enemies, let your light shine stuff?

Kid 1: Yeah. It's hard.

Kid 2: It would be impossible on our own.

Kid 1: It's a God thing.

Kid 2: And a friend thing. If you mess up, I'll be sure to let you know.

Kid 1: Thanks, you're a pal.

Kid 2: And I'll pray for you.

Kid 1: Really? That rocks.

Kid 2: That's built on the rock, man.

So that's how it looks to live the way Jesus taught. Let's see if you've got the picture.

Toss the four numbered balls to different parts of the room. Bring the kids with the balls to the front one-by-one and ask these questions. Allow kids to get help from the group if they need it. After each correct answer, let kids drop the ball into a bag.

Who has ball #1?

■ Tell about a time you've seen Christians "let their light shine" so people knew they were followers of Jesus.

■ Do you think it's fair for Jesus to ask us to love people who are mean to us? Explain.

■ Since God already knows all your needs, what's one thing you can stop worrying about?

■ How can you encourage your friends to build their lives on the rock of Jesus' words?

This is pretty radical stuff, isn't it? Loving your enemies just isn't the most natural thing in the world to do. What Jesus teaches us here is hard! And we can't manage it on our own.

Bible Verse
Let your light shine before men, that they may see your good deeds and praise your Father in heaven. Matthew 5:16

The people who listened to Jesus that day thought it was hard, too. They wanted to hear more of what Jesus had to say so they could learn how to do it. Jesus was with them—they could watch his life and listen to his words and learn from him. Now we have all of Jesus' life written down in the Bible. We don't have to meet on a crowded hillside to listen to him.

When I try to "let my light shine" on my own, I fall flat on my face. So will you. But when I let Jesus change me, I can start to live the way he wants me to. How do you let Jesus change you? Ask him to forgive your sins. Then trust him with your life. Tell him you believe in him and ask him to fill your heart with his love. You'll be amazed at what happens!

Today in your shepherd groups you'll learn how you can let Jesus' light shine through your life.

Dismiss kids to their shepherd groups.

② Shepherd's Spot ....

Gather your small group and help kids find Matthew 5 in their Bibles.

We call these three chapters in Matthew "the Sermon on the Mount." Today we just barely got our toes into the amazing things Jesus taught the people that day on the hillside. Distribute the "Words to Live By" handout. **You'll find all the passages from today's Bible story on this handout. It's pretty nifty. Cut out the two pieces on the heavy lines. Fold the right side to the center, and then fold the left side to the center. Wrap the small piece around the larger one and—voila!—you've got a mountain that grows.**

Ask volunteers to read each of the passages. **I need two or three of you to take each passage and work out a mini skit that shows how you might live out what Jesus taught. Make your skits as true-to-life as you can: something that might happen at home, in your neighborhood, on a sports team, or at school. I'll give you about three minutes to get ready.**

As kids prepare, offer help and ideas. Then ask each group to perform. Congratulate them on a good job!

■ **Which of these teachings of Jesus is the hardest for you to obey?**

■ **Can you think of some people who love their enemies and let their light shine? How do they do it?**

Happily, Jesus doesn't expect us to be able to live like this on our own. When we trust him with our lives, he changes our hearts and helps us glow with his love. Let's ask him to do that right now.

Give kids time to share prayer concerns, then close with a prayer similar to this one. **Dear Jesus, we want to do all the things you ask us to do, but we know we can only do them with your help. Enter our hearts today and fill us up with your love. I pray for** (mention each child's request). **Thank you for being our loving Savior, amen.**

Words to Live By

"You are the salt of the earth...You are the light of the world. Let your light shine before men, that they may see your good deeds and praise your Father in heaven." Matthew 5:13-14, 16

"You have heard that it was said, 'Love your neighbor and hate your enemy.' But I tell you: Love your enemies and pray for those who persecute you, that you may be sons of your Father in heaven." Matthew 5:43-45

house on sand. The rain came down, the streams rose, and the winds blew and beat against that house, and it fell with a great crash." Matthew 7:24-27

Glue center of smaller section here.

"Everyone who hears these words of mine and puts them into practice is like a wise man who built his house on the rock. The rain came down, the streams rose, and the winds blew and beat against that house; yet it did not fall, because it had its foundation on the rock. But everyone who hears these words of mine and does not put them into practice is like a foolish man who built his

"Therefore I tell you, do not worry about your life, what you will eat or drink; or about your body, what you will wear. Is not life more important than food, and the body more important than clothes? Look at the birds of the air; they do not sow or reap or store away in barns, and yet your heavenly Father feeds them. Are you not much more valuable than they? But seek first his kingdom and his righteousness, and all these things will be given to you as well." Matthew 6:25-26, 31

Words to Live By for

Workshop Wonders

In today's story Jesus teaches us that we are the salt of the earth and the light of the world. Whew! We need God's help to be a Christ-light—an example of God's love for everyone to see.

Set out the materials listed above on a covered table. Have each child take a cup. **Do you think you can let the light of Jesus' love bubble up and shine through you? Let's do a simple science experiment to see how that might happen.**

Have kids take turns pouring 1/2-inch of vegetable oil into their cups. If you choose, cover the cups with plastic wrap.

Pick up your cup and look at the oil. The oil is clear enough to see through. Walk your cup over to a window or hold it carefully up to the light. The oil catches the light, making it seem brighter and clearer. Have a volunteer read Matthew 5:13–16.

■ **When have you seen someone shine with Jesus' love?**

Have kids remove the plastic wrap and carefully pour a 1/4-inch layer of salt on top of the oil.

Jesus talked about salt in today's story. Salt adds flavor to whatever food it touches. Think how much flavor salt adds to the flavor of French fries or pretzels.

■ **How do God's people add "flavor" to the world?**

Now comes the tricky part. Sometimes we feel like being selfish or getting back at people who've made us mad. When all those nasty, selfish feelings come to the top, they dim God's loving light in our lives. Carefully pour water down the inside of your cup so you don't disturb the layer of salt at the bottom. Keep filling your cup with water until it's almost full.

Watch your kids' reaction as they observe bubbles of "bright" oil break through the salt crust and rise to the surface of their cups.

When we pray and ask God to "sink" our selfish feelings, his love rises to the top. We really need God's help to shine for him. No matter how hard we try to be like Jesus we can't quite manage. But when we ask God to help us, he changes our hearts—then we can shine like lights in a dark world. This week, ask God to help you shine for Jesus!

Fold down the corners to start your paper airplane.

SPECIAL DELIVERY

TO

Let your light shine!

Today at church we heard what Jesus told his followers about how to live. "Jesus tells us to love our enemies. How is that possible?"

Name two people who let the light of God's love shine in their lives.

"Therefore everyone who hears these words of mine and puts them into practice is like a wise man who built his house on the rock" (Matthew 7:24-29). Collect a large smooth rock from your yard. Scrub it clean and let it dry. Use a permanent marker to write Matt. 7:24-29 on the rock. Now add some moss! Mix 2 Tbsp. liquid starch, 2 Tbsp. water, 1/2 cup salt and two drops of green food coloring in a bowl and paint your rock.

Bible Verse

"Let your light shine before men, that they may see your good deeds and praise your Father in heaven."
Matthew 5:16

◊ What does it mean to build your life on the rock?

◊ What's one new way we can put Jesus' words into practice this week?

Family FUN

Live It!

The Very Big Little Lunch

Get Set
LARGE GROUP ■ Greet kids and do a puppet skit. Schooner is hungry to hear about leftover bread and fish.

❏ *large bird puppet* ❏ *puppeteer*

1 Bible 4U! Instant Drama
LARGE GROUP ■ "Bag Man" tells what happened when his young master shared his lunch with Jesus.

❏ *1 actor* ❏ *copy of pp. 50-51, Bag Man script* ❏ *4 numbered balls*
Optional: ❏ *large burlap bag*

2 Shepherd's Spot
SMALL GROUP ■ Create a "Care Package" to look for ways God shows his care. Share concerns and pray together. Send home the Special Delivery handout.

❏ *Bibles* ❏ *pencils* ❏ *scissors* ❏ *glue sticks* ❏ *copies of p. 54, Care Package* ❏ *copies of p. 56, Special Delivery*

Workshop Wonders
SMALL GROUP ■ Make and share Prayer Pretzels as promises to care for one another.

❏ *refrigerated bread or breadstick dough* ❏ *oven* ❏ *baking sheet* ❏ *water glass* ❏ *small plate* ❏ *coin* Optional: ❏ *egg* ❏ *pastry brush* ❏ *salt* ❏ *dipping sauce*

Bible Basis John 6:5-14 Jesus feeds 5,000 people.

Learn It! Jesus cares about people.

Live It! Show that you care.

Bible Verse For he is our God and we are the people of his pasture, the flock under his care. Psalm 95:7

Quick Takes

John 6:5-14

When Jesus looked up and saw a great crowd coming towards him, he said to Philip, "Where shall we buy bread for these people to eat?"

6 He asked this only to test him, for he already had in mind what he was going to do.

7 Philip answered him, "Eight months' wages would not buy enough bread for each one to have a bite!"

8 Another of his disciples, Andrew, Simon Peter's brother, spoke up,

9 "Here is a boy with five small barley loaves and two small fish, but how far will they go among so many?"

10 Jesus said, "Make the people sit down." There was plenty of grass in that place, and the men sat down, about five thousand of them.

11 Jesus then took the loaves, gave thanks, and distributed to those who were seated as much as they wanted. He did the same with the fish.

12 When they had all had enough to eat, he said to his disciples, "Gather the pieces that are left over. Let nothing be wasted."

13 So they gathered them and filled twelve baskets with the pieces of the five barley loaves left over by those who had eaten.

14 After the people saw the miraculous sign that Jesus did, they began to say, "Surely this is the Prophet who is to come into the world."

Insights

It's a spring day just before the Passover feast. Grass is greening over a mountainside along the north end of the Sea of Galilee. Jesus looks up and sees a mass of humanity coming toward him. Some come from curiosity, others to be healed, still others who simply long to sit in the presence of God's own Son and hear his winsome message.

As Jesus fed their souls, he remained acutely aware of their need for physical food as well. Jesus knew the tug of a growling stomach and the grind of fatigue. And he cared—not just for his close circle of friends but for the masses who clung to him. No wonder the people loved Jesus. He fulfilled their longings on every level. In fact, this "free lunch" inspired some to think of making Jesus their king. A lesser man might have taken this opportunity to seize power. But Jesus would be Lord of a spiritual kingdom, not an earthly one.

Kids are "whole people," just like the people Jesus fed. They come to your teaching time with all kinds of needs. Some may have witnessed a blow up between Mom and Dad on the way to church. Some may have suffered abuse; others might be dealing with growling tummies of their own because they dawdled and missed breakfast.

How wonderful for them to learn that Jesus cares about their every level of need. He sees them not as one of a mass, but as precious individuals who are worthy of his time and care. And as he cares for them, he wants them to care for others. A shared lunch, a listening ear, a word of encouragement from the Bible—these are all things your kids can offer as they learn to model their lives after the Savior.

Option Get Set

Well, look who dropped in today. I'm glad to see you! Every week when you come in, it just lights up my heart. You know why? Because you're special to me, and I have some wonderful things from God's Word just for you! Schooner's glad to see you too, aren't you, Schooner? *Schooner pops up.*

Schooner: *(rests head on leader's shoulder)* I am. They're great kids, aren't they?

Leader: You look a little, a little…

Schooner: Hungry! Got any birdseed?

Leader: *(check your watch)* It's not even close to lunchtime.

Schooner: I joined the Early Bird Brigade this morning and flew the 20K wingathon. I'm so hungry!

Leader: Hmm. I must have slept through it.

Schooner: It was a pretty fast fly by.

Leader: Oh, that explains it.

Schooner: I'd settle for a few breadcrumbs.

Leader: To find your way home?

Schooner: People scatter breadcrumbs, boss, birds have birdstinct.

Leader: You mean instinct, don't you, Schooner?

Schooner: "In" for you; "bird" for me.

Leader: Birdstink, huh? *(pinch nose)* If you insist.

Schooner: Hey!

Leader: Speaking of breadcrumbs, you'd have gotten plenty of them if you'd been at the picnic in today's Bible story.

Schooner: Really? They had picnics back in Bible times?

Leader: You bet they did. People came to a grassy hill to hear Jesus speak. And they didn't want to leave even when their tummies grumbled for food.

Schooner: Jesus was that good, huh?

Leader: Better. When Jesus spoke, miracles happened.

Schooner: What's a miracle?

Leader: A miracle is something that only God can do. Like changing a few loaves of bread into enough bread to feed 5,000 people.

Schooner: That's impossible, boss.

Leader: Nothing is impossible with God. And he cares about people.

Schooner: *(sigh)* Baskets of leftovers as far as the eye can see…

Leader: It would have fed your entire wingathon, and then some!

Schooner: Yum! I would've peck-peck-pecked until the cows came home.

Leader: No cows in this story, Schooner. But there were two small fish. So be sure to add fish heads to your menu.

Schooner: Fish? Mmm. If I had lips I'd lick 'em!

Leader: Jesus turned two fish into enough to feed the entire crowd.

Schooner: A miracle, right?

Leader: You catch on quick, Schooner.

Schooner: Of course, boss. I've to birdstinct, remember?

Leader: *(rub nose)* How could I forget?

Schooner: So dinner was a little bread…a little fish. I get it. Fish sticks!

Leader: Well, that's one way to look at it.

Schooner: Pass the tartar sauce. I'm ready to hear the whole Bible story!

Leader: Coming right up, Schooner, in Bible 4U!

1 Bible 4U!

Welcome to another exciting performance of Bible 4U! Theater—where Bible stories come to life before your very eyes! Before we begin today's story, I want you to be hungry. Be very, very hungry. You started the morning with a hike and now it's late in the day. You haven't had lunch—not even a granola bar. You're sitting on a grassy hillside with thousands of other people—kind of like being at a concert. Only this time the main attraction is Jesus himself!

Instant Prep
You'll need one person to play the role of "Bag Man." It can be you, or a good reader you choose from class. Your actor will need a copy of the "Bag Man" script, pp. 50-51.

The sun crossed the middle of the sky long ago and it's dipping toward the west. Your stomach is growling. You're hoping the people sitting next to you don't hear it. What's really hard is, you have a lunch sitting in a bag on the ground beside you. But many of the people around you have nothing to eat at all. You don't want to be rude and eat in front of them. So your stomach growls on and on...

But that's as far as I'm going with this story, because we have an important guest who was an eyewitness. In fact, he was the lunch bag I just mentioned. So, ladies and gentlemen, let's welcome Bag Man!

for Overachievers
Wrap your "Bag Man" in burlap to resemble a Bible time carrying bag. Or create a large burlap bag for the actor to step in. He/she can jump to the center of the storytelling area, as in an old-fashioned sack race.

Bag Man
Based on John 6:5-14

Hel-l-lo there! I'm Bag Man, the singing lunch bag. What, you've never heard of a singing lunch bag before? Well, that's why you come to church—to learn new things! New things about Jesus, that is.

And I can tell you something about Jesus. Oh, yeah. I can tell you a whole lot about Jesus. Know why? Because I'm not any old lunch bag. Oh-h-h, no. I'm the lunch bag that was there the day Jesus fed 5,000 people.

Sings to the tune of "I'm a Little Tea Pot."
I'm a little lunch bag on a string,
I'm off to a picnic, my fav'rite thing.

Five little loaves and two small fish,
As nice a lunch as a boy could wish.

Yup—that's me. The most famous lunch bag in all of history. Who cares about a lunch bag, you may ask. Well, lemmetellya, a WHOLE LOT OF PEOPLE cared about me the day I was brought to Jesus.

But, as you may have noticed in my song, I'm no empty bag. No sirree. So what's inside of me?

(Let kids respond—five loaves and two fish.)

What a smart bunch! So I need five of you to come up here and be loaves. *Select five volunteers. Hand them a ball of twine and have them tie themselves in a "bundle" just below the elbows.* Good! Now how about two fish? *Have the fish volunteers tie themselves together as well.* Excellent! Now you loaves and fishes, how about waving to the audience? *Pause as they wave.* Friendly little loaves and fish, aren't they? They're my supporting cast.

I belong to a boy named Nathaniel. He likes to go places, you know what I mean? Not a stay-at-home kind of kid. This morning he heard that Jesus was close by and he begged to go. Who wouldn't want to go see Jesus?

I mean, he heals sick people wherever he goes. And the way he teaches about God—it's a lot different from what we usually hear.

Nathaniel's mom said he could go. She said she would pack him a lunch, and told him to be home before dark. Woohoo! I knew we were off for an adventure. But I had no idea just how much of an adventure.

Nathaniel's mom picked me up (raise one shoulder) and shook me out *(shake your head from side to side.)* Then she stuffed me with five warm loaves—wave, guys—and two little fish. Flap your fins, fishies!

Nathaniel slung me on a string over his shoulder and off we went. Jesus and his disciples had gone away to rest, but we just followed the crowds and found them. Jesus welcomed all of us—thousands of people—and climbed up on a mountainside to teach. You should have heard him teaching about how God loves us. People just couldn't get enough of it.

As the day stretched toward evening, I could hear Nathaniel's tummy growling. I wondered why he didn't reach for me with my five loaves—wave, guys—and

my two little fish. Then I figured it out. Most of the other people didn't bring food. And Nathaniel didn't want to eat in front of them. He's a kid who really cares.

Well, guess what—Jesus cares too. Nathaniel wiggled through the crowd until he got pretty close to Jesus. We could hear the disciples talking with Jesus about how to feed all these people. There was no food anywhere in sight. Except for me, of course, and my five loaves *(signal them to wave)* and my two fish. That wouldn't go far, unless it was in Jesus' hands.

And that's exactly where I ended up! Nathaniel tugged on the sleeve of one of the disciples. "Hey!" he said. "I have a little lunch here that I could share." One little lunch for all those people? Right.

Jesus took me in his hands. Imagine—me in the hands of the Son of God! He took the loaves, gave thanks, and broke them into pieces. And more pieces, and more pieces! Then he did the same thing with the fish. Everyone sat down on the grass and ate until they were full.

(Let a select group of kids approach the loaves and fish as if they're about to devour them!)

Then the disciples gathered twelve baskets of leftovers!

I can't believe I had a part in such a super-wonderful miracle. All because Jesus cared about the hungry people, and Nathaniel was willing to share his lunch. You know, if you care about people, Jesus might do something amazing with you too!

Whoa—I hear Nathaniel coming for me.

(Raise your shoulder as if you're being picked up.)

I guess we're off on another adventure. Bye!

Bible 4U!

Let's hear it for Bag Man. And how about some appreciation for the loaves and fish? Now let's see if you have this story in the bag—and in your brains. Toss out the four numbered balls to different parts of the room.

Stand up if you have ball #1. Bring the kids with the balls to the front one by one and ask these questions. Allow kids to get help from the group if they need it. After each correct answer, let kids drop the ball into a bag.

■ **Why did thousands of people come to see Jesus?**

■ **What do you think Nathaniel told his mother when he got home?**

■ **Why didn't the boy in the story eat his lunch?**

■ **Think of two ways Jesus showed that he cared about people.**

Congratulations—you learned a lot about this story today!

You know, it can be hard to share things that are impor-tant to us. And food is important, especially when I'm tummy-rumbling hungry. It's pretty amazing that Nathaniel chose to share his lunch with Jesus. Can you imagine how it must have felt to see your little lunch multiplied to feed a huge crowd?

When we trust Jesus with our lives, we know that he will care for us. Psalm 95:7 says, "For he is our God and we are the people of his pasture, the flock under his care." It's great to know you're cared for. Then you can turn around and care for others, just like the boy in our story.

Today in your shepherd groups, you'll have fun learning what it means to be cared for. What a great feeling! And you'll bag a few ideas about how to pass that care on to others!

Dismiss kids to their shepherd groups.

Bible Verse
For he is our God and we are the people of his pasture, the flock under his care.
Psalm 95:7

2 Shepherd's Spot

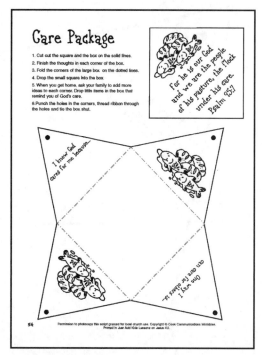

Gather your small group and help kids find John 6 in their Bibles.

Today we heard Bag Man tell the story we call "The Feeding of the Five Thousand." Now let's read it straight from God's Word. Have volunteers take turns reading John 6:5-14.

Wow—that was quite a picnic! God's people had been waiting hundreds of years for the Messiah God had promised. Seeing this miracle convinced them that Jesus was the one they'd been waiting for. The people felt so happy to have someone who would care for them, watch over them, and point the way to God.

Distribute the Care Package handout and ask a volunteer to read Psalm 95:7.

■ **How did Jesus show the people on the hillside that they were part of his flock?**

Check out this question on your handout: I know Jesus cares for me because... Jot down your ideas. Give kids a minute to record their thoughts, then have them share their ideas.

Now think about how you can care for others. Put a couple of ideas in the box on your handout, then we'll share them out loud.

Let kids share their ideas, then help them cut and fold their Care Packages.

One cool thing we learn from this story is that Jesus cares about everything in our lives— even the times when we're hungry. You can pray and talk to Jesus about anything that's important to you. What would you like us to pray about today?

Listen to each child's concerns, then close with prayer. **Dear Jesus, we understand that you care for us—that you even know when we're feeling hungry. Because we know how much you care for us, we bring you these things that are important to us.** (Pray for the children's concerns). **As we receive care from you, help us pass it on to others. In Jesus' name, amen.**

Care Package

1. Cut out the square and the box on the solid lines.

2. Finish the thoughts in each corner of the box.

3. Fold the corners of the large box on the dotted lines.

4. Drop the small square into the box.

5. When you get home, ask your family to add more ideas to each corner. Drop little items in the box that remind you of God's care.

6. Punch the holes in the corners, thread ribbon through the holes and tie the box shut.

For he is our God and we are the people of his pasture, the flock under his care.
Psalm 95:7

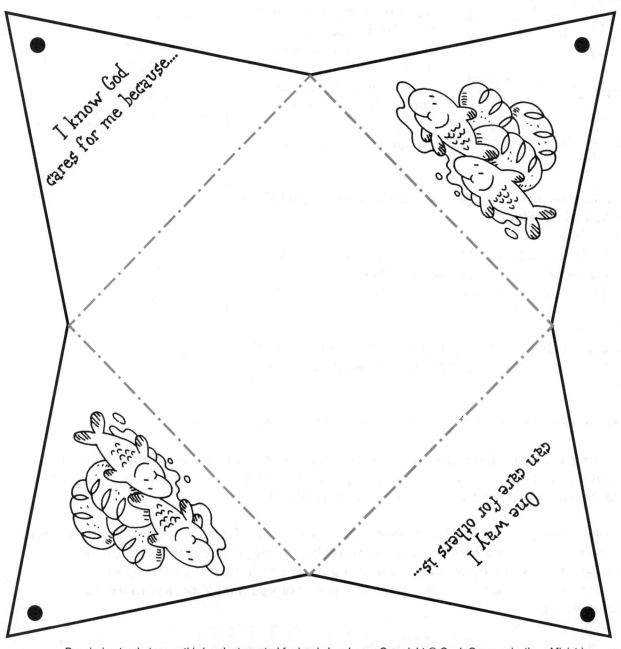

I know God cares for me because...

One way I can care for others is...

Workshop Wonders

I'm going to say a word and you tell me the first thing that comes to your mind. Ready? Pretzel. Let kids respond.

Do you know what I think of? Prayer. Really! Pretzels and prayer go back more than a thousand years. Monks in Italy used to bake scraps of dough in shapes that represented a child's arms folded in prayer—like this. Cross your arms over your chest to demonstrate. **Now that we're in the know, let's make Prayer Pretzels and serve them to church friends. This is one small way we can follow Christ's example and show we care for the people around us.**

Make sure everyone starts with clean hands! Set out refrigerated dough for bread or breadsticks. (If you're really ambitious, you might mix your own dough, or let your breadmaker do it for you.) One batch of dough should be enough for about eight kids. Divide the dough among kids and have them roll their pieces into a thick rope-shape, then fold them into pretzels. If you wish, brush them with beaten egg and sprinkle with coarse salt. If you're using yeast dough, let the pretzels rise for 10 minutes. Then bake according to the directions on the package.

Get List:
- ❏ refrigerated dough
- ❏ baking pan
- ❏ oven
- ❏ napkins

Optional:
- ❏ egg
- ❏ pastry brush
- ❏ coarse salt
- ❏ white paper
- ❏ water glass
- ❏ small plate
- ❏ coin

As we wait for our pretzels to bake, let's do an experiment that gives us an important clue about how to care for others.

Set out a sheet of paper, a coin, a glass of water and a small plate or saucer. Place the coin on the sheet of paper. Fill the glass with water and "sit" it on the coin. Have your kids take turns looking down through the water to see the coin. **To care for others, we have to watch out for opportunities that are right under our nose.** Set the small plate or saucer on top of the glass.

Now try to find the coin by looking through the glass. Pause as kids try to find the disappearing coin. **From some angles the coin will be visible. From other angles—poof!—it disappears.** Light reflection and the bending of light rays is the reason the coin seems to disappear and reappear.

Don't let this happen to you! When you see a need—put on the speed!—and do what you can to show others you care.

■ **Name a fun 'n' silly thing you might try to show someone you care.**

■ **What shall we say to people as we share our pretzels with them today?**

Let kids sample some of the pretzels and share the others. As they leave, remind them: **Like Jesus and the little boy who shared his lunch, look for ways to show people you care! Even the smallest thing can make someone's day. Give it a try!**

Fold down the corners to start your paper airplane.

SPECIAL DELIVERY

TO

Today we learned how Jesus fed a huge crowd on a hillside.

Why were there so many hungry people?

What "ingredients" did Jesus use for this lunch?

Jesus cares about people.
Show that you care!

Make "bread" ice cream to remember today's miracle story. Place a large scoop of ice cream on a sheet of waxed paper. Fold the waxed paper in half and use your hands to mold the ice cream into a mini-loaf of bread. Peel off the paper and set the loaf on a plate sprinkled with a mixture of granola and crushed nuts. Sprinkle more on top. Cover lightly with plastic wrap and freeze for one hour.

Bible Verse

"For he is our God and we are the people of his pasture, the flock under his care.
Psalm 95:7

Bite into your snack as you read John 6:5–14 from your Bible.
◊ When has God cared for our family in a special way?
◊ It's a wonderful life! Name three wonderful ways your life is better because your family cares for you.
◊ What is one of your favorite ways to care for others?

Family FUN

Live It!

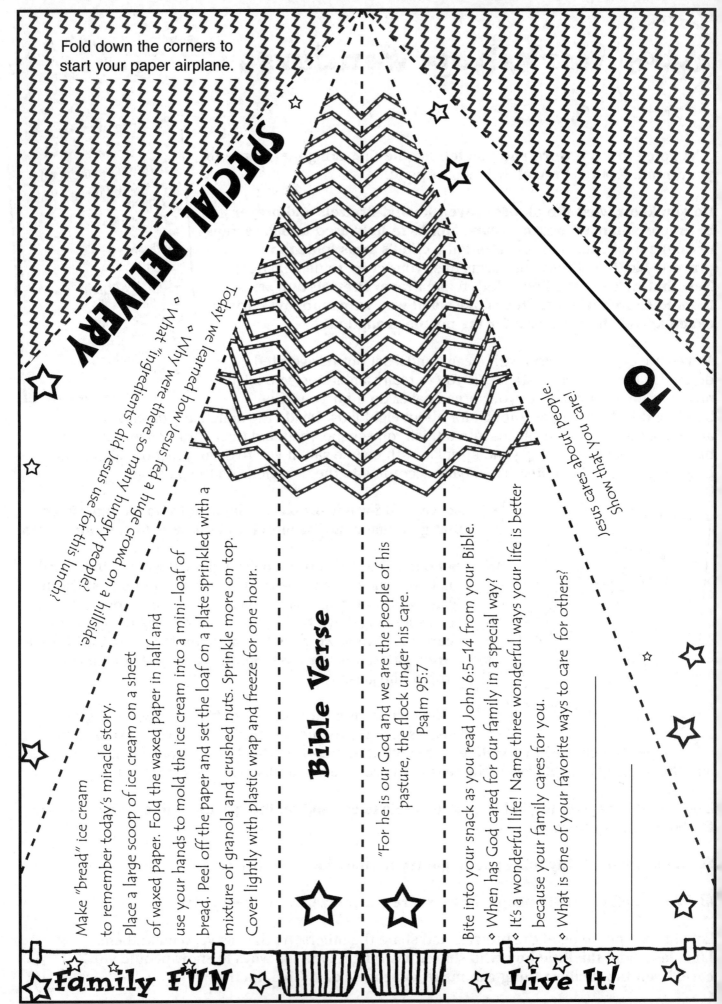

Storm Stopper

Get Set

LARGE GROUP ■ Greet kids and do a puppet skit. Schooner is hungry for a fish dinner until he hears about what happens in a storm.

❏ large bird puppet ❏ puppeteer

Bible 4U! Instant Drama

LARGE GROUP ■ Who better to tell the story of Jesus calming the storm than the Sea of Galilee itself?

❏ 1 actor ❏ copies of pp. 60–61, Storm at Sea script ❏ 4 numbered balls
Optional ❏ blue poster board ❏ blue ribbons

Shepherd's Spot

SMALL GROUP ■ Use the "Storm Stopper" handout to help kids believe that Jesus' awesome power is with them in all the storms of life. Share concerns and pray together. Send home the Special Delivery handout.

❏ Bibles ❏ pencils ❏ scissors ❏ copies of p. 64, Storm Stopper
❏ copies of p. 66, Special Delivery

Workshop Wonders

SMALL GROUP ■ Use two-liter bottles and hair dryers to blow up some science fun on fear and faith.

❏ two-liter bottles (drained and dried) ❏ hair dryers ❏ scraps of paper
❏ utility knife and cutting board

Bible Basis
Jesus calms the storm.
Mark 4:35–41

Learn It!
Jesus is all powerful.

Live It!
Trust in Jesus' power.

Bible Verse
Neither height nor depth, nor anything else in all creation, will be able to separate us from the love of God that is in Christ Jesus our Lord.
Romans 8:39

Quick Takes

Mark 4:35-41

That day when evening came, he said to his disciples, "Let us go over to the other side."

36 Leaving the crowd behind, they took him along, just as he was, in the boat.

37 A furious squall came up, and the waves broke over the boat, so that it was nearly swamped.

38 Jesus was in the stern, sleeping on a cushion. The disciples woke him and said to him, "Teacher, don't you care if we drown?"

39 He got up, rebuked the wind and said to the waves, "Quiet! Be still!" Then the wind died down and it was completely calm.

40 He said to his disciples, "Why are you so afraid? Do you still have no faith?"

41 They were terrified and asked each other, "Who is this? Even the wind and the waves obey him!"

Insights

The Sea of Galilee (sometimes called Lake Gennesaret or the Sea of Tiberius) provides the backdrop for much of Jesus' ministry.

This pear shaped lake, thirteen miles long and seven miles across, stretches along the Jordan Rift between the mountains and the Mediterranean Sea. The Jordan River, fed by springs and snowmelt from Mt. Hermon, flows into the north end of the lake, and drains from the south end toward the Dead Sea.

Because of his immense popularity in Galilee, Jesus often took to the lake to seek respite from the crowds who hungered for his teaching, his healing and his miracles. In this story, an obviously exhausted Jesus curled up on a cushion in the stern of the boat and fell fast asleep.

Several of Jesus' disciples were Galilean fishermen. No strangers to the fierce storms that struck the lake, these seasoned sailors knew just how to battle the ferocious winds that battered their sails when the warm, humid air of the Mediterranean met the cool mountain winds. But this storm overwhelmed them.

As wave after wave swamped the wooden boat, the disciples found their faith floundering as well.

Kids will be quick to identify with the disciples' terror as they struggled to survive the storm's fury. Day after day on TV, the Internet, and newspaper headlines, kids see evidence of overwhelming power. Much of it is evil—some imagined, but most very real. With the limited scope of childhood and not having the Son of God standing physically at their sides to speak and quiet the terror, kids feel helpless, at sea in a world awash with storms of terrorism and evil.

The truths in this lesson will reassure your students that they are linked by faith to the most unstoppable force in the universe—the power, in fact, that created the universe. And this power is unleashed by love, a love from which nothing can separate them. Use this lesson to reassure your kids that Jesus is as close to them as he was to the disciples that evening, that he loves them tremendously, and that his power is far greater than anything that can threaten them.

Get Set

Open your time together with kids' favorite action songs. **Hey, it looks like everyone is warmed up and ready to go. Are we missing someone?** *Schooner pops up.*

Schooner: Hi, boss.

Leader: *(rub Schooner's shoulders)* Hello, Schooner. It's a pleasure to rub shoulders with you again.

Schooner: Aw, shucks.

Leader: I have a question for you.

Schooner: Shoot.

Leader: Do you like the water?

Schooner: If you're talking a beach with palm trees and a clear blue sea with yummy fish swimming around, the answer is yes.

Leader: So you like swimming?

Schooner: Actually, I like fishing.

Leader: Ah, then you'll like today's Bible story.

Schooner: It's got fish?

Leader: It's got people who fish. And a boat.

Schooner: What kind of a boat? Something with a nice big rail for me to perch on?

Leader: Not exactly. This was a small wooden fishing boat with a sail.

Schooner: Cool! I love sailboats. Skimming over the water, swooping down to catch a mouthful…

Leader: Hold it, Schooner. This boat didn't actually skim over the water.

Schooner: It didn't? How come?

Leader: This was a working boat, designed to stay steady when the fishermen pulled in their heavy nets.

Schooner: Nets full of fish?

Leader: You bet.

Schooner: Mmm…a smorgasbord!

Leader: Do you ever stop thinking about your stomach?

Schooner: Only when I'm full.

Leader: I see. Well, catching fish isn't always an easy job, you know.

Schooner: Why not? You sit out on a lake in a nice little boat, throw in a net and the fish swim into it. What's so hard about that?

Leader: Weather.

Schooner: Weather?

Leader: Storms—big storms that rock the boat. Waves that wash right over it.

Schooner: Ooh. That doesn't sound fun at all.

Leader: Jesus' disciples would probably agree with you.

Schooner: They got caught in a storm?

Leader: Sure did. But they were lucky.

Schooner: Lucky? I don't think it's lucky to be caught in a storm in the middle of the lake.

Leader: I guess that depends on who's with you in the boat.

Schooner: You mean they had some hearty fishermen who knew how to sail the boat right out of the storm? *Heave ho, laddies! Pull, me hearties!*

Leader: Nope. This storm was too much even for the fisherman.

Schooner: That sounds bad. They must have been scared.

Leader: No doubt.

Schooner: So what happened? Did they…

Leader: They made it through okay. The storm stopped.

Schooner: All by itself?

Leader: Definitely not.

Schooner: *(irritated)* You're being awfully mysterious, boss.

Leader: Well I guess we'd better get straight into the Bible story and find out what happened.

Schooner: I guess so! I think I should've brought my webbed booties.

Leader: Webbed booties?

Schooner: Is there an echo in here? I wear them to help me swim. They're stylin'!

Leader: I'm sure.

Schooner: Let's get on with it, then!

Leader: Hang on, everybody—it's going to be a wet one! Here comes Bible 4U!

1 Bible 4U!

Have the Sea actor enter and stand by you. **Do you see what I see? It's a sea, if I've ever seen one. Makes quite a scene, doesn't it! But this isn't any old sea, you see. It's the Sea of Galilee.** Sea waves. **Nice waves!**

If you've read very many stories about Jesus, you know that he spent a lot of time around the Sea of Galilee. The first four disciples he chose were fishermen from its fishing villages. Jesus found a friendly **welcome almost everywhere he went on Galilee's shores.** Sea nods.

That's one reason we've asked the Sea of Galilee to join us today. It has first-hand knowledge of some of the most exciting stories from Scripture. Sea gives the "okay" sign.

Jesus even liked to go to the sea for getaways. So let's get ready for a little cruise. But look lively—you never know what the next wave might bring!

Storm at Sea
Based on Mark 4:35–41

I bet you've heard of me. I'm the Sea of Galilee. I sit smack in the middle of the land of Israel. I'm here to tell you about an amazing thing that happened over two thousand years ago. Before I get ahead of myself, let me tell you a little more about me.

I lie in a big basin almost 700 feet below the sea level. That's like a 68-story building! I'm full of fresh water from the Jordan River that flows into me up here *(point north)* and drains me down here *(point south)*. And I'm full. Full of fish! Boatloads of fish.

There's only one problem with fishing here—the weather. Every now and then it pitches a fit. But it's not my fault. You see, the Mediterranean Sea isn't very far away. And the weather there is a lot different from the cool, dry weather in the mountains above me. When the wind funnels through the hills and those two weather systems clash—KABOOM! We have a storm.

Not just a few sprinkles, mind you. Winds rip across and stir up waves that nearly swamp the boats. It can get SO nasty SO fast. I'll show you.

Everybody raise your hands to eye level and make gentle little ripples with your fingers. This is a nice day with a little wisp of a breeze tickling my surface. Wiggle as if you're being tickled. Ooh—that feels so good!

Now that cool breeze from the mountains is starting to drift down. Pull your elbows out to the side at shoulder height and make bigger waves. That's right—things are getting a little choppy. Okay, drop your arms.

Things are getting worse by the second. The warm, humid air from the sea just started to mix it up with the cool wind from the mountains. My waves are out of control. Starting at this side (indicate one corner of the room), do the wave. Now do it again, faster. Now faster!

Whew! Talk about rocking your boat. No one can stay afloat in weather like this. And that's exactly what happened on the day I want to tell you about.

Jesus had been teaching people near my shore. When evening came, he and his disciples climbed into a boat to sail across me. Jesus was tired. He went to one end of the boat and lay down to sleep. It was a calm, lovely evening. Make the little ripples with your hands in front of your eyes.

Then that cool mountain wind started to blow. Bring your elbows out to the side for bigger waves. Who can tell me what happened next? Pause for an answer. Right! The mountain breeze hit the hot air from the sea, and I got all riled up. Do the wave from this way to that way. Now that way to this way. Now back again.

There was lighting and thunder and rain and that fishing boat with Jesus and the disciples was rockin' and rollin'. I didn't want to pitch anyone out the boat, but with a storm like that; there was nothing I could do. The disciples were scared out of their skin! Wave after wave washed over the boat. Lighting crackled, thunder boomed, and it looked like all was lost.

So where was Jesus while all this was happening? Sound asleep on a cushion at the back of the boat. In desperation, the disciples woke him up. "Teacher!" they cried. "Don't you care if we drown?"

Jesus did care. He stood up and said to the storm, "Quiet! Be still!" Just like that (snap your fingers) the wind stopped and my surface grew calm. Spread your hands palms down in front of you and move them back and forth to show my calm surface.

As the fishing boat continued its journey, the disciples stared at Jesus, open-mouthed. Turn to a neighbor and exchange open-mouthed stares. Pause. Wow! You guys do that really well!

Seeing that the wind and waves obeyed Jesus, the disciples were pretty freaked out. I mean, it's not like you see somebody stop a storm every day. Nope—they knew Jesus was more than a man. He was the very Son of God!

I've always been blown away by the storms that rock my surface. But I've never seen anything like the power Jesus showed when he calmed the storm. From thunder and lightning and crashing waves to absolute stillness, just like that!

Cup your hands in front of you. Think of your hands as Jesus' hands. Think of yourself, cradled safely right there in the palm of his hand. Jesus is all-powerful, and you are in his care. Nothing can ever separate you from his love. How cool is that!

The sea exits.

Whoa—that was some pretty serious storm action we had going there. I'm glad Jesus stopped it! I wonder if you were able to learn anything in the middle of all those choppy waves. Let's see.

Toss the four numbered balls. Call the kids who catch the balls one-by-one to answer these questions. Let them ask help from the audience if they need it.

 ■ **Why did Jesus need an evening getaway?**

 ■ **What do you think scared the disciples most—the storm, or the way Jesus stopped the storm? Explain.**

 ■ **You're one of the disciples. It's the morning after Jesus calmed the storm. What do you say to your friends?**

 ■ **What did the disciples learn about Jesus from this miracle?**

Sometimes Jesus did miracles in front of huge crowds—like when he fed thousands of people from one boy's lunch. Some miracles Jesus did just in front of his disciples.

Even though there was a small "audience" when Jesus calmed the wind and the waves, the message about his power is for all of his followers, for all time. So listen up. There's nothing in the whole universe that can match Jesus' power. Nothing at all. **Name some of the most powerful things you know.** *Pause for responses.* **Do you think that can match Jesus' power? No way! No how! Not even close!**

Jesus didn't do this miracle just to flex his power muscles. He did it so that his disciples would learn to trust his power, and his love for them. In your shepherd groups you'll learn how that power works in your lives. So get going!

Dismiss kids to their shepherd groups.

Bible Verse
Neither height nor depth, nor anything else in all creation will be able to separate us from the love of God that is in Christ Jesus our Lord. Romans 8:39

2 Shepherd's Spot

Gather your small group and help kids find Mark 4:35–41 in their Bibles.

We find lots of exciting stories in the book of Mark. It's the shortest of the four Gospels—books about Jesus' life. Mark has a way of getting right to the adventure. And there's certainly a boatload of adventure in this story!

Have volunteers take turns read the passage aloud.

■ **What were the disciples thinking as Jesus slept?**

Do you know what's cool? Jesus is with us today every bit as much as he was with the disciples in this story. We don't see him, but we do see evidence that he's there. Let's see how to look for Jesus' power.

Distribute the Storm Stopper handout, p. 64. Have kids turn the handout face down, fold the sides to the middle, then cut away the portion above the waves.

■ **What does this look like to you?** (Jesus' hand stopping the storm.)
■ **When do you need to trust in Jesus' power to control the things that are happening around you?**

Ask a volunteer to read Romans 8:39 from the handout.

■ **What does this verse say to you?**

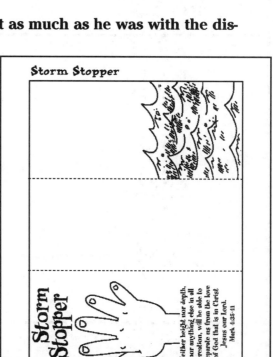

Storm Stopper

Storm Stopper

Neither height, nor depth, nor anything else in all creation, will be able to separate us from the love of God that is in Christ Jesus our Lord.
Mark 4:35-41

64   Permission to photocopy this script granted for local church use. Copyright © Cook Communications Ministries. Printed in Just Add Kids Lessons on Jesus 4U.

Storm Stopper

See the blank section in the middle of your Storm Stopper? Use that to write a message to Jesus to tell him that you trust in his power. Later, when you take it home, you can have everyone in your family sign their names. They can even add their own messages of trust.

Let kids share what they wrote. Then invite them to share other things they'd like to pray about. Listen carefully to their concerns, reassuring them that Jesus is more powerful than all their problems and scary situations. Close with prayer. **Dear Jesus, sometimes our world feels stormy. The things we see on the news and the things that happen in our families seem so power-filled and scary. Help us remember that you are more powerful than anything, and that you hold us right in the palm of your hand, amen.**

Storm Stopper

Storm Stopper

Neither height nor depth, nor anything else in all creation, will be able to separate us from the love of God that is in Christ Jesus our Lord.

Mark 4:35-41

Workshop Wonders

We hear that the disciples were totally scared in today's story.

■ **Based on today's Bible story, what was the disciples' top fear?** (Drowning.)

Yes! Being washed out of the boat and lost in the storm was a major worry. We can imagine, too, having the waves push us far, far away from the safety of the boat and the wind howling so that no one could hear our cries. I'm sure the disciples thought, "If only we can hold on and stay inside the boat, we'll make it."

■ **When have you been as afraid as the disciples were that day?**

■ **What kept you afloat?**

Fear filled the disciples' hearts, pushing away their trust in Jesus. The fear factor was high, the trust factor but a drop in the bucket! The disciples learned a great lesson that day: It wasn't the boat that would save them—it was Jesus' power over nature.

■ **What rocks your boat when you're at home? At school?**

Let's do a little experiment with fear and faith. Lay the 2-liter bottles on their sides on the floor. Place them near electrical wall outlets. Have kids gather around the bottles. Hand one in each group the hair dryer. (Hair dryers use lots of power. Stay on the conservative side so you don't blow a circuit.)

The hair dryer represents the windy storm that tossed the disciples' boat on the Sea of Galilee. The disciples wanted to make it to the shore—to safety. Let's say the empty bottles represent the safety of the shore. Each of you wad a little piece of paper to represent a tiny boat. One at a time, place your tiny boats near the mouth of the bottle. Use the hair dryer to blow the boat to safety out of the storm and into the bottle. Let the storms blow!

After several kids have tried to get their boats in the bottles, call time. Explain: Because the bottles are already filled with air, pushing in more guarantees no room for the little boats. **Suppose the air in the bottle represents our fear. When our hearts are filled with fear, it chokes out our faith!**

■ **How did the disciples replace their fear with faith?**

■ **What can you learn from their experience?**

Carefully slice off the top third of each bottle with a utility knife. **Let's get rid of the fear that chokes out our faith. This time, when you blow your little boats to safety, point the nozzle of the hair dryer slightly away from the bottle. This will help your little boats scoot right in.** As kids blow their boats, have helpers hold the bottles steady.

So we got rid of our fear, and we pointed the nozzle away. That's like looking at Jesus and what he can do instead of looking at how terrible the storm is. With Jesus in charge, the disciples' small wooden boat became a powerboat! There's no need to fear, when Jesus is near. His power is greater than anything. To close, review Romans 8:39 with your kids.

Fold down the corners to start your paper airplane.

SPECIAL DELIVERY

TO

Trust in Jesus' power to help.

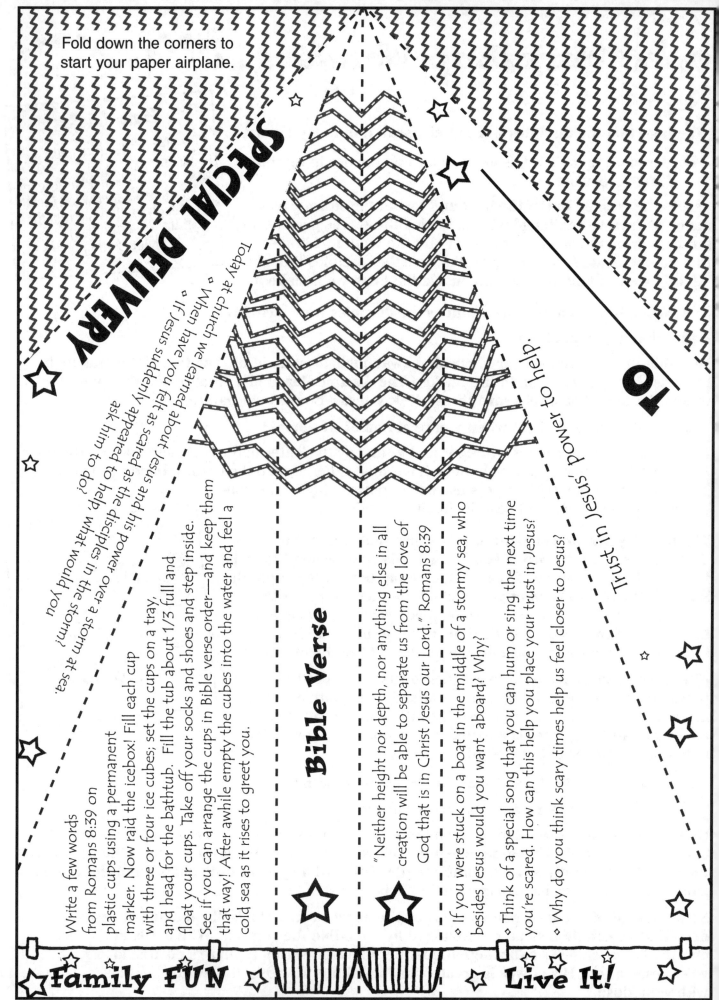

Today at church we learned about Jesus and his power over a storm at sea.

"When have you felt as scared as the disciples in the storm?"

"If Jesus suddenly appeared to help, what would you ask him to do?"

Family FUN

Write a few words from Romans 8:39 on plastic cups using a permanent marker. Now raid the icebox! Fill each cup with three or four ice cubes; set the cups on a tray, and head for the bathtub. Fill the tub about 1/3 full and float your cups. Take off your socks and shoes and step inside. See if you can arrange the cups in Bible verse order—and keep them that way! After awhile empty the cubes into the water and feel a cold sea as it rises to greet you.

Bible Verse

"Neither height nor depth, nor anything else in all creation will be able to separate us from the love of God that is in Christ Jesus our Lord." Romans 8:39

Live It!

◊ If you were stuck on a boat in the middle of a stormy sea, who besides Jesus would you want aboard? Why?

◊ Think of a special song that you can hum or sing the next time you're scared. How can this help you place your trust in Jesus?

◊ Why do you think scary times help us feel closer to Jesus?

Good Sam

Option

Get Set
LARGE GROUP ■ Greet kids and do a puppet skit. Schooner remembers showing kindness to his grandmother.

❏ large bird puppet ❏ puppeteer

1

Bible 4U! Instant Drama
LARGE GROUP ■ Two teachers of the law find a special challenge in Jesus' story of the Good Samaritan.

❏ 2 actors ❏ copies of pp. 70–71, Won't You Be His Neighbor? script
❏ 4 numbered balls Optional ❏ Bibletime costumes

2

Shepherd's Spot
SMALL GROUP ■ Use the "Emergency Care" handout to help kids think about practical ways they can show kindness.

❏ Bibles ❏ pencils ❏ scissors ❏ copies of p. 74, Emergency Care
❏ copies p. 76, Special Delivery

Option

Workshop Wonders
SMALL GROUP ■ Party hats and ribbon make "Help in a Hat" pick-me-ups for a friend.

❏ paper party hats ❏ colored tissue paper ❏ packets of lemonade mix
❏ chocolate coins ❏ animal cookies ❏ zip-top bags Optional: ❏ ribbon
❏ construction paper ❏ hole punch ❏ white board

Bible Basis – Luke 10:25–37

Learn It! God cares when people hurt.

Live It! Show kindness.

Bible Verse Always try to be kind to each other and to everyone else. 1 Thessalonians 5:15

Quick Takes

Luke 10:25–37

On one occasion an expert in the law stood up to test Jesus. "Teacher," he asked, "what must I do to inherit eternal life?"
26 "What is written in the Law?" he replied. "How do you read it?"
27 He answered: "'Love the Lord your God with all your heart and with all your soul and with all your strength and with all your mind'; and, 'Love your neighbor as yourself.'"
28 "You have answered correctly," Jesus replied. "Do this and you will live."
29 But he wanted to justify himself, so he asked Jesus, "And who is my neighbor?"
30 In reply Jesus said: "A man was going down from Jerusalem to Jericho, when he fell into the hands of robbers. They stripped him of his clothes, beat him and went away, leaving him half-dead.
31 A priest happened to be going down the same road, and when he saw the man, he passed by on the other side.
32 So too, a Levite, when he came to the place and saw him, passed by on the other side.
33 But a Samaritan, as he traveled, came where the man was; and when he saw him, he took pity on him.
34 He went to him and bandaged his wounds, pouring on oil and wine. Then he put the man on his own donkey, brought him to an inn and took care of him.
35 The next day he took out two silver coins and gave them to the innkeeper. "Look after him," he said, 'and when I return, I will reimburse you for any extra expense you may have.'
36 "Which of these three do you think was a neighbor to the man who fell into the hands of robbers?"
37 The expert in the law replied, "The one who had mercy on him." Jesus told him, "Go and do likewise."

Insights

If you're looking for the all-time champions of one-upmanship, look no further than the experts in the law from Jesus' time. Rather than obeying the spirit of the law which taught "love your neighbor as yourself," they preferred endless debates of fine details such as the very question this man asked Jesus: "Who is my neighbor?" Believing that devout Jews should keep themselves apart from foreigners, they wanted to make sure they didn't spread the love too far!

Jesus was a burr in the side of these experts. They saw him as a young, upstart rabbi from "nowheresville," and his popularity with the people had them miffed. So they tried to discredit him by challenging him with difficult questions in public. If they could trip him up, he might lose his following. "What must I do to inherit eternal life?" was a particularly loaded question. The wealthy, powerful Sadducees claimed there was no eternal life. The more numerous Pharisees taught that people who didn't believe in eternal life would be shut out of the kingdom of heaven. Jesus' answer was bound to alienate one group or the other.

But Jesus cut through to the heart of the issue. By making the despised Samaritan the hero, he demonstrated the shallow, uncaring attitudes of the priest and Levite. In what must have been a shocking story, Jesus enlarged the boundaries of God's care.

Like the Jews of Jesus' day, it feels risky for a child to step out of his or her social circle to show compassion. Use this lesson to help your kids understand that God cares about all people: the kid who sits alone in the lunch room, the last to be chosen for a team, the person who smells bad, the one who struggles to communicate in English. Loving them is not an option—it's at the very core of God's commandments.

Get Set

Let kids warm up with songs that allow them to get the wiggles and giggles out and help them focus on praise. **Good morning, all you lovely people! I'm glad to see all your happy faces. We're going to have a good time in God's Word today. Hey—has anyone seen a parrot around here?** *Schooner pops up.*

Schooner: *(sings)* I feel pretty, oh so pretty. I feel pretty and witty today!

Leader: You're in a good mood, Schooner.

Schooner: Does it show?

Leader: When you're happy, the whole world smiles with you.

Schooner: *(tries to smile)* Can you see my smile, boss?

Leader: *(takes a look)* No. But I know you're happy.

Schooner: *(shakes head)* It's not easy being...ah...lip-less.

Leader: Sorry, Schooner.

Schooner: *(hangs head)*

Leader: *(have the group give a collective "aw-w-w." Give Schooner a hug.)* And when you're hurting the world gets a much different picture.

Schooner: It's the pits, boss.

Leader: I understand.

Schooner: When a bird's beak hits a pit...oi!

Leader: *(rub Schooner's beak)* You must get a lot of that, you poor thing.

Schooner: It's pitiful. Really.

Leader: Well, Schooner, when people hurt, God cares.

Schooner: I'm glad.

Leader: And when people hurt, God wants us to care for them too.

Schooner: Works for me, boss.

Leader: It's called kindness.

Schooner: I know! I know! Like the time I helped Granny Bird when she flew into that plate glass window. Splat! That was an ugly sight, lemme tell ya'.

Leader: Is she okay, Schooner?

Schooner: Oh, sure, boss. Granny never flies without her seat belt.

Leader: Granny wears a seat belt?

Schooner: And her helmet. It sure helped that day.

Leader: Hmm. If you say so, Schooner.

Schooner: I made some of my special bird's nest soup. Helps every time. Pretty soon Granny was back to her old self. Flying high!

Leader: Grandmas, grandpas, friends. Let's always be on the look out for someone who needs a helping hand.

Schooner: ...or wing!

Leader: Chicken wings. I love 'em!

Schooner: What's that?

Leader: Tender loving care when it's needed most—that's what makes God smile.

Schooner: Like this? *(Schooner tries to smile again.)*

Leader: umm...yes!

Schooner: *(excitedly)* Did I do it that time?

Leader: I can see a smile in your eyes!

Schooner: Smilin' eyes...

Leader: It's one of the things I love about you, Schooner.

Schooner: Aw, shucks, boss.

Leader: And how you help me each week. *(Have the group give Schooner a round of applause.)*

Schooner: I'm here to help. Squawk!

Leader: By the way I have a new song for you.

Schooner: I love to sing!

Leader: It's called, "Turkey in the Straw."

Schooner: Wait a minute. Are you calling me a turkey, boss?

Leader: Never!

Schooner: Bird jokes. Grrrrrr. On to Bible 4U!

1 Bible 4U!

Welcome to Bible 4U! I have a question for you, and I'll be surprised if anyone can answer "no." Did you ever pick a fight? Not a smack-em-up kind of fight—an argument. Like when you drop a few nasty jabs or say something that makes the other guy feel embarrassed.

I bet you're not mean enough to do that very often. But the people in today's Bible story were. And do you know who they liked to pick fights with? Jesus! You see, Jerusalem was full of people who were experts in God's law. But they weren't really loving people like you might expect them to be. They were picky, picky, picky. And they were really jealous of all the attention Jesus was getting. So, when Jesus was teaching, they'd join the crowd and then ask Jesus a question to see if they could trip him up.

Instant Prep
Before class, ask two volunteers who are good readers to play the roles of Amos and Micah. Give them copies of "Won't You Be His Neighbor?" (below) to review.

for Overachievers
Have two actors from your drama team prepare this story. Give them Bible costumes and beards made from faux fur.

As you might be able to guess, that didn't work out so well for them. Because Jesus saw right past the tricky questions and into their hearts that were unloving and cold. On this particular day, Jesus answered all questions with a story. And it didn't turn out quite as the teacher of the law expected. Let's listen in as he talks it over with one of his friends.

Won't You Be His Neighbor?
Based on Luke 10:25-37

Micah: Hey, Amos, what's goin' on? You look a little down.

Amos: Oh, Micah, I didn't see you. Yeah, I'm down. If I were anymore down my chin would be dragging on the street.

Micah: What's goin' on?

Amos: I just had a close encounter with that new rabbi in town.

Micah: You mean Jesus? The one from Nazareth?

Amos: That's the one.

Micah: Isn't it amazing how people follow him around?

Amos: It is. It's like they've forgotten that we're the experts here.

Micah: I know—it's so annoying. Today I was listening to him and I thought, "Micah, here's your opportunity to embarrass this guy with a question he can't answer."

Amos: Oh—I like the sound of that. So what did you ask him?

Micah: I said, "Teacher, what do I have to do to get eternal life?"

Amos: And he said?

Micah: He asked a question back. "What is written in the Law?"

Amos: Well that's easy! "Love the Lord your God with all your heart and love your neighbor as yourself."

Micah: Yeah, that's exactly what I said. So he says to me, "That's the right answer. Do that and you'll live."

Amos: So he came off looking like the expert and you felt pretty dumb.

Micah: Oh, man, did I. And it made me mad.

Amos: And then?

Micah: I came back with another question. A harder one this time.

Amos: Really. What did you ask?

Micah: I asked, "But who's my neighbor?"

Amos: Ooh—good one. I bet Jesus didn't have a quick answer to that one. I mean, we could argue about that for days!

Micah: You're right. It wasn't a quick answer. It was a really long answer. And it rocked my world.

Amos: Huh?

Micah: He told a story.

Amos: A story? What kind of a story?

Micah: A story about a man who was traveling down the road to Jericho.

Amos: That's a nasty road—full of robbers.

Micah: Uh-huh. And the man was attacked and robbed and beaten up.

Amos: That happens on that road pretty often. If I remember right, it's a really narrow road that winds along a canyon. There are all kinds of places robbers can hide. It's not the kind of place you want to travel alone.

Micah: So this guy is lying by the road, hurt and bleeding. He can't move.

Amos: He was in bad shape, huh?

Micah: Uh-huh. Then a priest comes down the road, but he walks right by.

Amos: Hmm.

Micah: And then a Levite goes by, but he doesn't help either.

Amos: Huh. He was probably in a hurry to get to the temple. We're not lookin' too good here, are we?

Micah: Nope. All this time the injured man is lying there. If nobody helped him, he would die. Then he hears more footsteps coming down the road.

Amos: Who is it this time?

Micah: A Samaritan.

Amos: A Samaritan? Yuck! We don't have anything to do with those guys. They don't believe in worshiping God the way we do or anything. I've walked miles out of my way to keep from going through Samaria.

Micah: The Samaritan stops to help the injured guy. He takes care of his wounds, puts the guy on his donkey and takes him to an inn. He pays the innkeeper to take care of the man. Jesus finishes this story, then asks me, "Which of these men was his neighbor?"

Amos: Ouch. You had to say that it was the Samaritan.

Micah: Exactly. Then Jesus said, "Go and do likewise."

Amos: There's no way to argue with that.

Micah: Nope. Jesus was right and I felt like a complete fool.

Amos: That's tough. But…what do you think about that? Does God expect us to treat people who aren't our friends like our neighbors? To be kind to people we don't even know?

Micah: That's what Jesus said. And I hate to admit it, but I think he's right.

Amos: Me too. I've always wondered if we're pickier than God wants us to be.

Micah: I've wondered that too. We're always telling people how they ought to live, but do we really love them?

Micah: Maybe that's why people follow Jesus. They can tell he cares about them. He shows them God's love like they've never seen it before.

Amos: Do you think we ought to go hear more of what Jesus has to say?

Micah: It couldn't hurt.

Amos: And maybe we ought to really listen instead of looking for ways to pick an argument.

Micah: Do you think we can do that? We were born to argue.

Amos: If we hang on to our tongues. *They both grab their tongues and hang on.*

Micah: Let's go.

Amos: I'm right behind you!

That's quite a turnaround that Micah and Amos did. Let's see if you caught what happened. Toss the four numbered balls to different parts of the room.

Bring the kids with the balls to the front one-by-one and ask these questions. Allow kids to get help from the group if they need it. After each correct answer, let kids drop the ball into a bag.

■ The teachers of the law didn't like Jesus—they picked arguments with him. Why?

■ If you're on the road to Jericho and you see a man who's been robbed and beaten, what would keep you from stopping to help?

■ Sometimes you see someone who needs help, but you have to be smart about staying safe. How can you help but still stay safe?

■ What kinds of "hurts" do people experience that we can't see?

The teachers of the law made a big show of doing the right thing. But they cared a lot about showing off and looking like they were right. They didn't care so much about people and their hurts. That's not the way God planned it. So Jesus straightened them out.

Jesus explained that God isn't impressed when we make a big deal out of doing good things. The way to please God is to show God's love to people, even when no one is looking. The religious men in Jesus' story were doing good things. They were hurrying to study and teach and take care of the temple. But they weren't doing the best thing. It didn't bother them to walk right by someone who desperately needed their help. Jesus doesn't want us to "walk right by." He wants us to be on the lookout for people who need a friend.

Bible Verse
Always try to be kind to each other and to everyone else.
1 Thessalonians 5:15

How do you do that? How can you be the kind of neighbor Jesus talked about? That's exactly what you're going to find out in your shepherd groups today.

Dismiss kids to their shepherd groups.

2 Shepherd's Spot

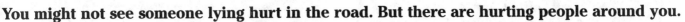

Gather your small group and help kids find Luke 10:25-37 in their Bibles.

Jesus had a wonderful way of teaching with stories. Instead of saying to the teachers of law, "You don't care about people at all!" he told the story of the Good Samaritan. Let's look carefully at our own lives and see how we can do what Jesus taught.

Have volunteers take turns reading Luke 10:25–37 aloud.

You might not see someone lying hurt in the road. But there are hurting people around you.

■ **What are ways people hurt that we don't see from the outside?**

Helping someone who's hurting may sound pretty compli-cated. But it doesn't have to be! I'll show you what I mean.

Pass out the "Emergency Care" handout. Have kids fold it in half and cut out the emergency light shape. Show them how to cut away the shaded center section, then fold it in half again to form a booklet. Let them write their names on the front of the booklet, then take turns reading the ideas on the inside.

■ **Which of these things do you think you could do?**

These are all simple things, but they can make a huge difference to someone who needs a helping hand. Hang onto this little booklet. Each time you try one of these ideas, write your initial on the hand beside it.

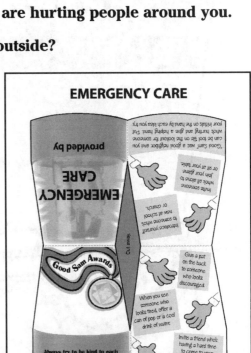

On the back, you'll find a Good Sam Award page.
Think of a couple of people who have given you hope and a helping hand when you really needed it. Write their names on this page.

Ask kids to share their concerns, then close with prayer. **Dear Jesus, we want to be good neighbors like the Samaritan in the story. And so today we pray for each other.** (Pray for each child by name). **Help us see the hurting people around us and reach out in your love, amen.**

EMERGENCY CARE

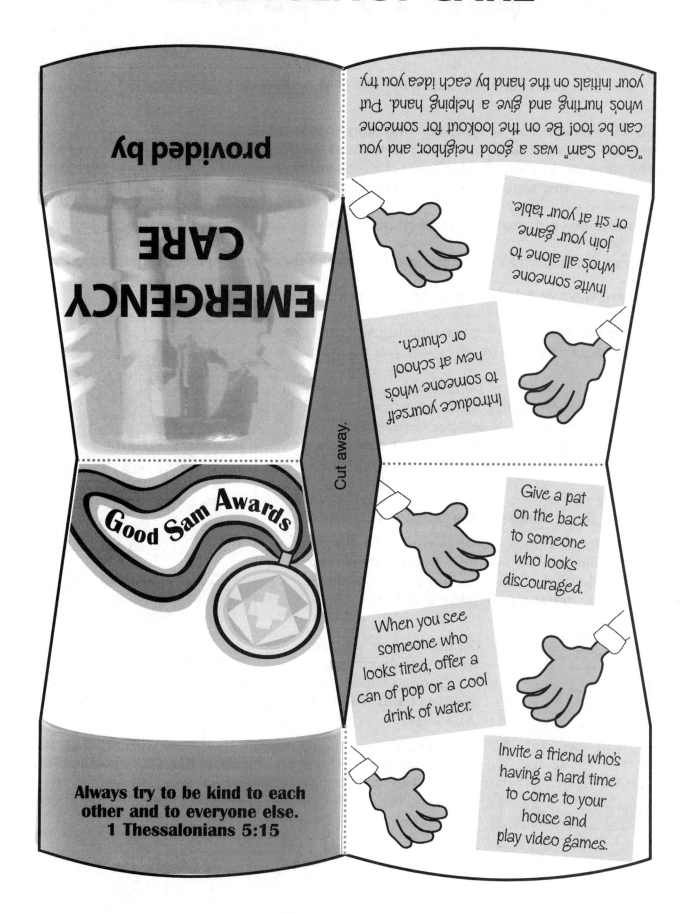

provided by

EMERGENCY CARE

Good Sam Awards

Always try to be kind to each other and to everyone else. 1 Thessalonians 5:15

"Good Sam" was a good neighbor and you can be too! Be on the lookout for someone who's hurting and give a helping hand. Put your initials on the hand by each idea you try.

Cut away.

Invite someone who's all alone to join your game or sit at your table.

Introduce yourself to someone who's new at school or church.

Give a pat on the back to someone who looks discouraged.

When you see someone who looks tired, offer a can of pop or a cool drink of water.

Invite a friend who's having a hard time to come to your house and play video games.

Workshop Wonders

Jesus wants his followers to show kindness—all day, every day, in places you might not think of! In today's story a man gets beaten and robbed and left to die. He wouldn't have made it unless someone stopped to help. But when two religious leaders saw the man, they walked on by. Finally a foreigner stopped and tended the wounded man, took him to an inn where he would be cared for, and even paid the bill.

■ **Suppose you were the injured man. What would you have prayed for?**

Maybe you can be someone's answer to prayer today. We're going to make "Help in a Hat" gifts that you can give to someone who needs a pick-me-up. Your gift might be just the right thing for someone who's hurting and discouraged.

Get List:
- ❏ paper party hats
- ❏ colored tissue paper
- ❏ packets of lemonade mix
- ❏ candy coins
- ❏ animal cookies
- ❏ zip-top bags

Optional
- ❏ construction paper
- ❏ stapler
- ❏ ribbon
- ❏ hole punch
- ❏ white board

Pass out the party hats. If you don't have party hats, let kids make paper cones from construction paper. Place a small piece of tape and then punch holes on each side and thread ribbon through the holes. Knot the ends of the ribbon to secure. Line the hat with colorful tissue paper.

Now let's see what helpful items we can put in our hats. Set out the packets of lemonade mix and let kids drop one or two in their hats. **Life can be sour. But a little kindness from Christian friends sweetens it up!**

Let kids put several animal cookies in zip-top bags and add them to the hats. **The Good Samaritan's donkey carried the wounded man to safety in today's Bible story. Your "beast of burden" may be a bike, and your friend who needs a little kindness could be a bike ride away!**

Spill chocolate coins onto the table. **The Good Samaritan was generous with his money. A few coins meant a warm bed and a hot meal for our wounded traveler.**

Let's finish by making a gift tag. You might want to say, "To: (your friend's name), From: a friend who cares. Maybe you want to sign your name, or perhaps you'd like to keep it a secret. On the back of the tag, you could add an encouraging Bible verse. Write this portion of Psalm 52:8 on a white board for kids to copy: "I trust in God's unfailing love for ever and ever."

Let kids discuss who will receive their "Help in a Hat" gifts and how they will deliver them. **Have fun being "Good Sams"!**

75

Fold down the corners to start your paper airplane.

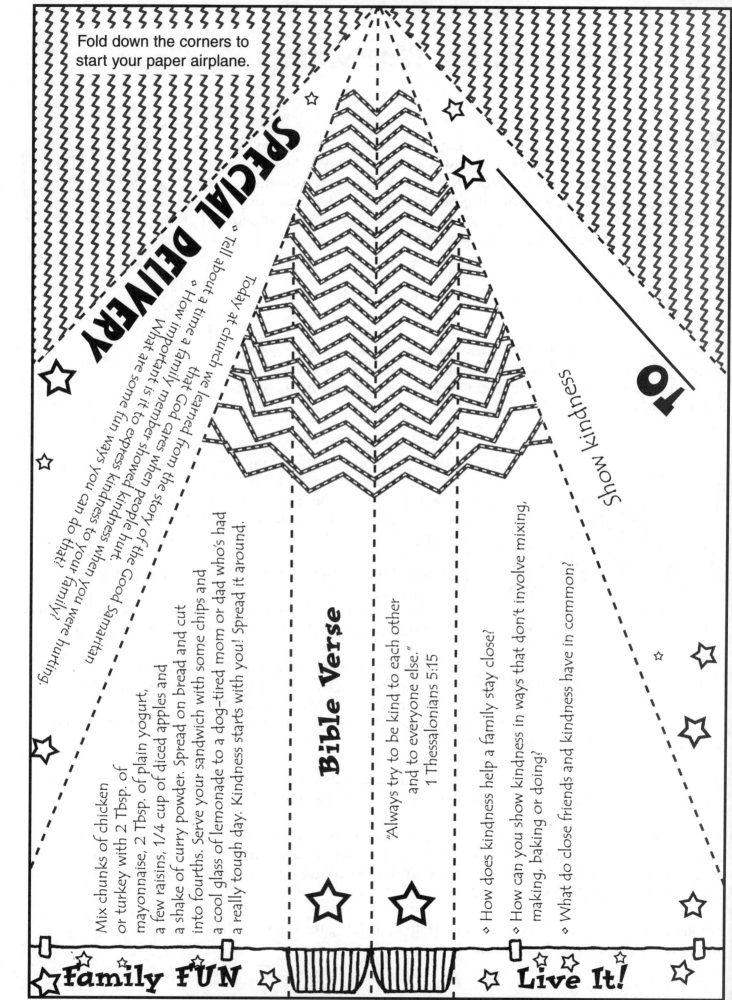

SPECIAL DELIVERY

TO

Show kindness

Today at church we learned from the story of the Good Samaritan that God cares when people are hurt. What are some fun ways you can express kindness when you or your family were hurting. How important is it to show people a Tell about a time a family member had. What are some fun ways you can do that?

Family FUN

Mix chunks of chicken or turkey with 2 Tbsp. of mayonnaise, 2 Tbsp. of plain yogurt, a few raisins, 1/4 cup of diced apples and a shake of curry powder. Spread on bread and cut into fourths. Serve your sandwich with some chips and a cool glass of lemonade to a dog-tired mom or dad who's had a really tough day. Kindness starts with you! Spread it around.

Bible Verse

"Always try to be kind to each other and to everyone else."
1 Thessalonians 5:15

Live It!

◊ How does kindness help a family stay close?

◊ How can you show kindness in ways that don't involve mixing, making, baking or doing?

◊ What do close friends and kindness have in common?

76

A Little Girl Lives

Option — Get Set
LARGE GROUP ■ Greet kids and do a puppet skit. Schooner's cold leads to a discussion of how Jesus healed a little girl.

❑ large bird puppet ❑ puppeteer

1 — Bible 4U! Instant Drama
LARGE GROUP ■ Jairus tells the moving story of the day he went to Jesus for help.

❑ 3 actors ❑ copies of pp. 80–81, She Lives! script ❑ 4 numbered balls
Optional ❑ Bibletime costumes ❑ backdrop and props for Galilean house

2 — Shepherd's Spot
SMALL GROUP ■ Use the "Hope Scope" handout to help kids understand that there's no such thing as a hopeless situation.

❑ Bibles ❑ pencils ❑ scissors ❑ copies of p. 84, Hope Scope
❑ copies p. 86, Special Delivery

Option — Workshop Wonders
SMALL GROUP ■ Use a rising science experiment to reinforce the point that Jesus helps when things appear hopeless.

❑ wide-mouthed jar with cork stopper ❑ funnel ❑ Alka-Seltzer® tablets
❑ sharpened pencils ❑ scissors ❑ glue ❑ bowl and spoon ❑ pitcher of water ❑ tissue paper ❑ index cards Optional: ❑ balloons ❑ index cards
❑ hole punch

Bible Basis Jesus raises Jairus's daughter. Mark 5:22–24, 35–43

Learn It! Jesus helps when things seem hopeless.

Live It! Hope in the Lord.

Bible Verse Be strong and take heart, all you who hope in the Lord. Psalm 31:24

Quick Takes

Mark 5:22–24, 35–43

Then one of the synagogue rulers, named Jairus, came there. Seeing Jesus, he fell at his feet

23 and pleaded earnestly with him, "My little daughter is dying. Please come and put your hands on her so that she will be healed and live."

24 So Jesus went with him. A large crowd followed and pressed around him.

35 While Jesus was still speaking, some men came from the house of Jairus, the synagogue ruler. "Your daughter is dead," they said. "Why bother the teacher any more?"

36 Ignoring what they said, Jesus told the synagogue ruler, "Don't be afraid; just believe."

37 He did not let anyone follow him except Peter, James and John the brother of James.

38 When they came to the home of the synagogue ruler, Jesus saw a commotion, with people crying and wailing loudly.

39 He went in and said to them, "Why all this commotion and wailing? The child is not dead but asleep."

40 But they laughed at him. After he put them all out, he took the child's father and mother and the disciples who were with him, and went in where the child was.

41 He took her by the hand and said to her, "Talitha koum!" (which means, "Little girl, I say to you, get up!").

42 Immediately the girl stood up and walked around (she was twelve years old). At this they were completely astonished.

43 He gave strict orders not to let anyone know about this, and told them to give her something to eat.

Insights

How desperate would a Jewish leader and highly respected member of the community have to be in order to publicly throw himself at Jesus' feet and plead for help? The dire illness of Jairus's daughter brought him to this point. Here he was, a member of the Jewish establishment, the one in charge of synagogue services and maintenance. But the prestige of his position melted in the anguish of his daughter dying.

Jesus was once again in the middle of a crowd by the lake, probably in the city of Capernaum, when Jairus broke through and pleaded for Jesus to come lay his hands on the dying girl "so that she will be healed and live."

Jesus went, but before they arrived messengers came from Jairus's house with word that the little girl was dead. Deep anxiety gave way to hopelessness and despair. They were too late. She was gone. In this moment of human extremity, Jesus displayed peace and confidence. Urging the father to keep believing, Jesus took Peter, James and John and proceeded to the house. Jeering mourners laughed out loud at Jesus' assertion that the little girl was only sleeping. In a matter of moments, Jesus had the little girl up and walking around. Derision turned to amazement.

The kids in your class know those feelings of hopelessness and despair. When their public or private world spins out of control, they feel as powerless as a matchstick on a stormy ocean. It can be a challenge even for adult "saints" to maintain quiet confidence in God's power in the face of awful, seemingly irreversible circumstances. But it is in these times, when we've reached the end of what's humanly possible, that we begin to feel some measure of God's omnipotence. Use this lesson to teach your kids that when we serve the living God, there's no such word as "hopeless."

Get Set

Wow! You guys look terrific this morning. I wish I could say the same for Schooner. I saw him looking a little peaked just a few minutes ago. Schooner? Are you there? *Schooner pops up.*

Schooner: Achoo!

Leader: Do you have a cold, Schooner?

Schooner: I don't…ahhh-choo! think so.

Leader: You seem to have the sniffles.

Schooner: But only when I…achoo!…sneeze.

Leader: A little R & R might help.

Schooner: Reading and writing?

Leader: Rest and relaxation.

Schooner: Maybe if you pinch my beak it would keep me from dripping and sneezing.

Leader: *(pinch puppet's beak)* Like this?

Schooner: Ow! Now my ears are plugged up. *(shakes his head to clear it)*

Leader: Just sneeze again and all should be fine.

Schooner: *(sneezes and hiccups loudly)* Now I've done it! *(hiccup!)*

Leader: Maybe you're allergic to something.

Schooner: Like what?

Leader: I don't know—people maybe. People can be allergic to birds, so maybe birds can be allergic to people.

Schooner: I doubt it. I was sneezing before you got here, remember?

Leader: Oh, yeah.

Schooner: I don't know what to do. I've gone through a whole box of tissues.

Leader: Do you know what people in Bible times did when they were sick?

Schooner: What?

Leader: They looked for Jesus. He healed people all the time.

Schooner: Did he take their temperature and give them lemon tea?

Leader: Not exactly. He did something much better than that. He took away their sickness and made them well.

Schooner: No way!

Leader: Yes way!

Schooner: How do you know that?

Leader: The Bible tells us. Jesus healed many people, even those close to death…even those who had already died.

Schooner: No!

Leader: Yes!

Schooner: Is there an echo in the room?

Leader: Could be.

Schooner: How did Jesus do that stuff?

Leader: With a powerful, heavenly touch. Jesus cared when he saw people hurting.

Schooner: Did Jesus help kids, or just grown-ups?

Leader: Today's Bible story is about a girl.

Schooner: Did she have the sniffles like me?

Leader: She was very, very sick, Schooner. Her father hoped with all his heart that Jesus could help her.

Schooner: *(pauses)* How did it turn out?

Leader: I'd hate to spoil the story.

Schooner: Ah-CHOO!

Leader: Ooh—that cold sounds pretty bad. What if I go fix you some nice chicken soup?

Schooner: Chicken soup! I'll have you know that chickens run in my family.

Leader: Oops. Turkey, then.

Schooner: Hey! I think your taste in soup is pretty fowl.

Leader: Maybe we'd better forget the soup and go for the story instead.

Schooner: I'm with ya' there.

Leader: All righty then. Let's have some hearty Bible 4U!—hold the chicken!

1 Bible 4U!

Today's instant drama finds us beside the Sea of Galilee again, probably in the town of Capernaum. Guess where Jesus is—in the middle of a crowd! Big surprise, eh? People just couldn't get enough of Jesus. Before he even set foot in a town, a crowd was there to greet him.

Over hundreds of years, God had sent many prophets to guide and help his people. Usually they came with warnings about what would happen if the people didn't follow God, and about the blessings that would come if they did.

Instant Prep

Choose a thoughtful reader to be Jairus, or play him yourself. Use a calm child to play Jesus. He has just a few lines. Rachel is a silent character who will wait at the side. Jesus and Jairus need copies of the script. Recruit two groups of kids to be mourners and the crowd. In a small class, use everyone in the two groups.

for Overachievers

Create a backdrop of the interior of a Galilean house at one side of your performance area. Add floor cushions, pottery and a plant. Create a palette on the floor where Rachel will lie. Dress the characters in Bible costumes. Call "extras" from the audience to be the crowd and the group of mourners.

Some of the prophets even did a miracle here and there. But there had never been anyone like Jesus. He spoke to the people with love and tenderness. When sick people came to him, he put his hands on them and instantly they got well. He fed the crowds when they were hungry. There was one thing for sure: Jesus cared about the people, and they knew it! That's why, in the hour of his greatest need, even a synagogue leader rushed to find Jesus. Let's listen to his story.

She Lives!
based on Mark 5:22–24, 35–43

Jairus: Such a day it was. My little girl had been sick—wasting away before our very eyes. Could she eat? No. Drink? Hardly a sip. Her brow was hot and dry, cheeks as pale as the clouds. Nothing we did could bring her out of her fever. I was desperate. I had heard of Jesus and his miracles. Hadn't he healed people all over Galilee? Calmed a storm? Cast out demons that no one else could touch?

I had thought of going to Jesus ever since Rachel got sick. But think of who I am—Jairus, the ruler of the synagogue. What does a synagogue ruler do, you ask?

Everything, that's what. I'm in charge of the all the services—who reads, who prays. I make sure the building is clean and well maintained. I'm a very important member of the community. If I asked help from Jesus, no matter how famous he was, there would be trouble from the Jewish community. Tongues would wag. I could lose my job. I was in a tough spot.

But Rachel grew sicker by the hour. Suddenly my job seemed not to matter at all. What did I care for being the ruler of the synagogue when my dear child lay on her bed, close to death? What would we do if we lost our beautiful Rachel? Her breathing grew shallow and ragged. All color drained from her face. My wife cried softly at her side—the end was near. That's when I decided I had to go to Jesus. He was our only hope, and Rachel's only chance at life.

Jesus and crowd enter. Crowd separates as Jairus breaks through.

It wasn't hard to find Jesus. He was near the lake in the middle of a crowd, as always. I had to get close to him—now! I pushed my way through the crowd and threw myself at his feet. People gasped. But Jesus looked at me with kindness in his eyes. "My little daughter is dying!" I cried. "Please come and put your hands on her so that she will be healed and live."

Jesus touches Jairus's shoulder kindly. Everyone moves toward Jairus's house.

Jesus didn't hesitate a moment. Of course, when we started for my house the crowd tagged along. Someone touched Jesus' robe and he stopped to see who it was. It was a woman who had been sick for years and years. Just by touching Jesus' clothes, she got well. Surely there was hope for my little girl too!

But just as we were turning toward my house again, messengers stopped us.

Messenger: Your daughter is dead. Why bother the teacher anymore?

Jairus: *(drooping)* At that moment, my hope just melted. It was awful. She was dead. We were too late. My little girl—my own sweet Rachel was gone. But Jesus' words broke through my thoughts.

Jesus: *(earnestly)* Don't be afraid. Keep on believing!

Jairus: *(to audience)* Keep on believing? They said Rachel was dead, so what's to believe? Still—I saw him heal the

woman in the street. Maybe there was hope. We kept going. When we got close to the house, we could hear the mourners wailing and crying loudly. But that didn't bother Jesus.

Pause for the mourners to perform. Jesus raises his hands to quiet them.

Jesus: Why all this commotion and wailing? The child is not dead but asleep.

Mourners laugh and point.

Jairus: The mourners laughed at him. So he sent them away and we went into the house.

Jesus points and sends them away, then beckons Jairus to follow him. They stand in front of Rachel who's lying still on the floor. Jesus takes her hand.

Jesus: Little girl, get up.

Rachel sits up, then rises to her feet and hugs her father.

Jairus: You can see with your very own eyes what happened. My daughter stood up and walked around! Everyone was astonished.

Crowd and mourners show amazement. Jesus, Jairus and Rachel stand in front of the class.

Jairus: All hope was gone—and then Jesus came. Only Jesus could have brought my little girl back to life. He can bring hope to your life when everything seems hopeless. *(to mourners)* Do you believe it?

Mourners: Yes!

Jairus: *(to crowd)* Do you believe it?

Crowd: Yes!

Jairus: *(to audience)* Do you believe it? *(Pause for response).* Good—because it's true. *(Pulls Rachel to the front.)* My daughter is living proof that Jesus can bring hope to any situation.

Once again, Jesus gives us a surprise ending, and a happy one! Let's see what important things you learned from this story. Toss the four numbered balls to different parts of the room.

Bring the kids with the balls to the front one-by-one and ask these questions. Allow kids to get help from the group if they need it. After each correct answer, let kids drop the ball into a bag.

■ **Why was it surprising that Jairus came to Jesus?**

■ **Suppose you were Jairus. What would you have done when the messengers said the little girl was dead?**

■ **What did you learn about Jesus from this story?**

■ **If you were the little girl, what would you have told your friends the next day?**

First Jairus felt desperate. He had to get to Jesus—no one else could save his little girl's life. Then, when the messengers came and said, "Your daughter is dead," Jairus must have felt hopeless and cold inside.

Bible Verse
Be strong and take heart, all you who hope in the Lord. Psalm 31:24

I bet we all know what hopeless feels like. Maybe there's an "F" on a test or a report card. Maybe Mom or Dad is gone. Maybe something terrible happens in our world and it seems like nothing will ever be the same again.

When those hopeless feelings wash over you, there's something I want you to remember—Jesus' words to Jairus. Do you remember them? Jesus said, "Don't be afraid. Keep on believing." Those words from Jesus are for us, too. Let's try saying them together. "Don't be afraid. Keep on believing." Ask God to help those words stick in your mind.

Today in your shepherd groups you'll discover some wonderful verses that will help you keep on believing!

Dismiss kids to their shepherd groups.

② Shepherd's Spot

Gather your small group and help them find Mark 5:22 in their Bibles. Have volunteers take turns reading Mark 5:22–24, 35–43.

Jairus, the man in today's story, found himself in a desperate situation. His little girl was really sick and he needed to do something quickly! He found Jesus, but a messenger told him his little girl had died. It must have been hard for Jairus, but he went along with Jesus. And before long, his little girl was up and walking again!

■ **What do you think Jairus learned about Jesus that day?**

I remember feeling like Jairus once. Share with kids a time when God helped you through a "hopeless" situation.

■ **If you could pick a color for the word "hopeless," what color would you choose? Why?**

When you're having a "hopeless moment," the most important thing you can do is remember that God is God, he loves you, and he can do anything! The Bible verses on our "Hope Scope" handout will remind you of all those good things.

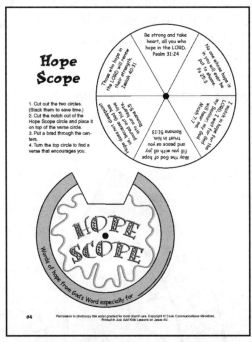

Distribute the Hope Scope handout. Show kids how to cut out and stack the Bible verse circle and the notched circle and fasten them with a brad. As they turn the notched circle, Bible verses will show through the notch. Let kids take turns reading the verses aloud.

Maybe you'd like to keep your Hope Scope for yourself. Or maybe you'd like to give it to someone who needs to know that Jesus helps when things seem hopeless. Have kids write the appropriate name in the blank on the front circle.

Jairus ran through the town to find Jesus, but we can talk to him anywhere, any time. Let's do it! Allow kids to share their prayer requests. **Dear Jesus, we can only imagine how Jairus felt when you brought his little girl back to life. When things feel hopeless, help us remember your incredible power. Right now we pray for** (mention each child's request). **Thank you for caring about us, both our insides and outsides, amen.**

Hope Scope

1. Cut out the two circles. (Stack them to save time.)
2. Cut the notch out of the Hope Scope circle and place it on top of the verse circle.
3. Put a brad through the centers.
4. Turn the top circle to find a verse that encourages you!

Be strong and take heart, all you who hope in the LORD. Psalm 31:24

No one whose hope is in you will ever be put to shame. Psalm 25:3

I watch in hope for the LORD. I wait for the God my Saviour; my God will hear me. Micah 7:7

May the God of hope fill you with all joy and peace as you trust in him. Romans 15:13

Hope does not disappoint us, because God has poured out his love into our hearts. Romans 5:5

Those who hope in the LORD will renew their strength. Isaiah 40:31

HOPE SCOPE

Words of hope from God's Word especially for _____

Workshop Wonders

Imagine laughing at Jesus as the crowd did in today's Bible story—pointing your finger at the Savior of the world and yelling, "The daughter of Jairus asleep? A lot you know, buster!" Today, as then, people do not trust Jesus to know what he knows. After all, experience teaches us not to trust someone who can't tell the difference between death and an afternoon nap. But, as always, Jesus knows the whole truth. Jesus helps when things seem hopeless. Let's place our trust in him.

You may wish to perform this experiment for the class and have kids lend a hand. Or have enough items on hands for kids to work in groups. Make a hole in the cork stopper by pushing through the sharpened pencil. Then gently push the funnel's end into the hole. Make sure the funnel fits tightly.

Get List:
- ❏ jar with cork stopper
- ❏ funnel
- ❏ Alka-Seltzer® tablets
- ❏ sharpened pencils
- ❏ scissors
- ❏ glue
- ❏ bowl and spoon
- ❏ pitcher of water
- ❏ tissue paper
- ❏ stickers
- ❏ Optional: balloons, index cards, hole punch

■ **What parts of today's raising-from-the-dead story miracle would you share with someone who didn't know anything about Jesus? Would they believe you?**

Make small tissue paper "girls" (3 per experiment) to represent the young girl in today's story. Trace the figure shown here. Carefully place a sticker on each figure. Fill the wide-mouth jar half-full with water.

■ **Today's Bible Verse states: "Be strong and take heart, all you who hope in the Lord." When would be a good time for you to remember that verse?**

Crush the Alka-Seltzer tablets and sprinkle them in the water. Quickly cover the jar with the cork-and-funnel stopper and rest the tissue paper girls in the funnel. **Watch what happens.** The girls will rise and float above the jar. Depending on the freshness of the seltzer tablets, you may need to add another tablet to the water

Option: If you prefer a simpler option for today's activity, gather balloons, colorful index cards and a hole punch. Make paper confetti using the hole punch and the index cards. Have kids pick a balloon, blow it up, and then rub it against their hair. Slowly bring the balloon close to the confetti. The paper will "rise" and appear to walk across the table.

As you go today, remember that trusting in Jesus means never giving up hope. He is all powerful, all wise, and he loves you very much!

Fold down the corners to start your paper airplane.

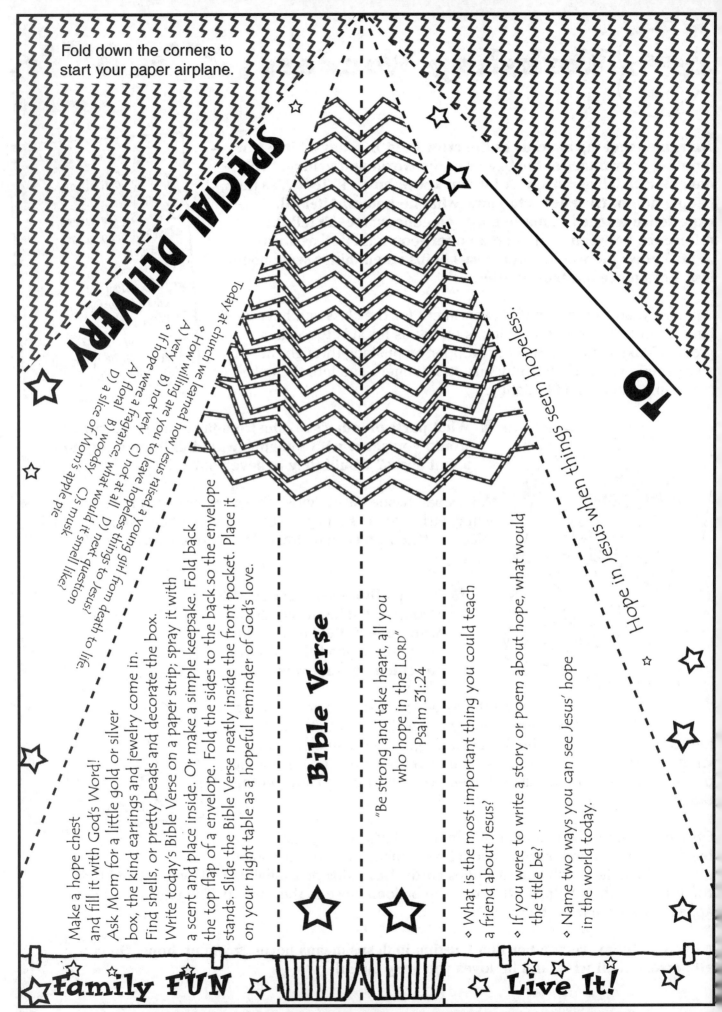

SPECIAL DELIVERY

TO

Hope in Jesus when things seem hopeless.

Today at church we learned how Jesus raised a young girl from death to life.

"If hope were a hopeless things to Jesus!

How willing are you to leave your hopeless things to Jesus!
A) very   B) not very   C) not at all   D) next question

"If hope were a fragrance, what would it smell like?
A) floral   B) woodsy   C)'s musk   D) a slice of Mom's apple pie

Family FUN

Make a hope chest and fill it with God's Word!

Ask Mom for a little gold or silver box, the kind earrings and jewelry come in. Find shells, or pretty beads and decorate the box. Write today's Bible Verse on a paper strip; spray it with a scent and place inside. Or make a simple keepsake. Fold back the top flap of a envelope. Fold the sides to the back so the envelope stands. Slide the Bible Verse neatly inside the front pocket. Place it on your night table as a hopeful reminder of God's love.

Bible Verse

"Be strong and take heart, all you who hope in the LORD"
Psalm 31:24

Live It!

◇ What is the most important thing you could teach a friend about Jesus?

◇ If you were to write a story or poem about hope, what would the title be?

◇ Name two ways you can see Jesus' hope in the world today.

Little Man in a Big Tree

Get Set
LARGE GROUP ■ Greet kids and do a puppet skit. Schooner finds out the truth of Jesus' love for people.

❑ large bird puppet ❑ puppeteer

Bible 4U! Instant Drama
LARGE GROUP ■ Zacchaeus tells how an encounter with Jesus changed his life.

❑ 2 actors ❑ large shirt or jacket ❑ copies of pp. 90-91, Go Climb a Tree script ❑ 4 numbered balls

Shepherd's Spot
SMALL GROUP ■ Use the "One, Two, Tree!" handout to record three ways to love difficult people like Zacchaeus.

❑ Bibles ❑ pencils ❑ scissors ❑ copies of p. 94, One, Two, Tree!
❑ copies of p. 96, Special Delivery

Workshop Wonders
SMALL GROUP ■ Edible fig trees reinforce the loving truth of today's Bible story.

❑ 8-inch wheat tortillas ❑ softened cream cheese ❑ shredded carrots
❑ chopped figs ❑ honey ❑ cinnamon ❑ celery tops ❑ large mixing cup and spoon ❑ plates and plastic knives ❑ extra cream cheese
Optional ❑ gummy candy figures

Bible Basis
Luke 19:1–10
Zacchaeus meets Jesus.

Learn It!
Jesus loves everyone.

Live It!
Show Jesus' love.

Bible Verse
We love because he first loved us.
1 John 4:19

Quick Takes

Luke 19:1-10

Jesus entered Jericho and was passing through.

2 A man was there by the name of Zacchaeus; he was a chief tax collector and was wealthy.

3 He wanted to see who Jesus was, but being a short man he could not, because of the crowd.

4 So he ran ahead and climbed a sycamore-fig tree to see him, since Jesus was coming that way.

5 When Jesus reached the spot, he looked up and said to him, "Zacchaeus, come down immediately. I must stay at your house today."

6 So he came down at once and welcomed him gladly.

7 All the people saw this and began to mutter, "He has gone to be the guest of a 'sinner'."

8 But Zacchaeus stood up and said to the Lord, "Look, Lord! Here and now I give half of my possessions to the poor, and if I have cheated anybody out of anything, I will pay back four times the amount."

9 Jesus said to him, "Today salvation has come to this house, because this man, too, is a son of Abraham.

10 For the Son of Man came to seek and to save what was lost."

Insights

Have you ever marveled at kids' expertise in name calling? There is hardly a derogatory name that wouldn't apply to Zacchaeus. As a chief tax collector, he would have been a big-time collaborator with the hated Romans. A crime boss of sorts. The Jews were at the mercy of the tax collectors. Zacchaeus's wealth undoubtedly came from charging a little (or a lot) extra and skimming the profits for his personal bank account. Since other tax collectors reported to him, he probably got a share of their "take" as well.

And he could hardly have had a more prosperous area to oversee. Situated on a major trade route, Jericho enjoyed a thriving economy. At 820 feet it's the worlds lowest city with an enviable "resort" climate. A literal oasis in the desert, fresh water springs kept it well watered and comfortable. Today, as in Bible times, fruit and vegetables grow there year round. Between trade and tourism, Zacchaeus would have had plenty of revenue to tax!

How scandalized the "good people" of Jericho must have been when Jesus singled out this miniature, mean, miserable man and announced a personal visit. It was unthinkable. Who wouldn't have reacted that way? Would your thoughts have been any different than the witnesses in the crowd that day long ago?

Use this lesson to help kids see that where Jesus is concerned, no one is a lost cause. And hating someone who seems to richly deserve it is not an option. God calls us to be "safe" people who will offer forgiveness and acceptance to anyone who seeks it. Jesus, of all people, could have looked down his nose at Zacchaeus.

Instead, he saw the desperately miserable heart of the man, took the initiative, and offered love. It's an example kids can follow: When others see a "loser," they can see both the pain and the potential for God's transforming love and forgiveness.

Get Set

Welcome! I'm glad to have your company this morning. Let's share a bit about Jesus' love for all those who have faith in him. Big people, little people and all of us in between. Schooner, fly on up and give me a hand, I mean, a wing! *Schooner pops up.*

Schooner: I'll help out on one condition.

Leader: What's that?

Schooner: No more chicken jokes.

Leader: Will do, my feathered friend.

Schooner: *(leans head on the Leader)* I love ya, boss.

Leader: …and Jesus loves us both.

Schooner: I knew that!

Leader: Jesus loves everyone. Big people. Even people who aren't very nice.

Schooner: Why would Jesus do that?

Leader: Because everyone needs to hear the Good News about him.

Schooner: Yeah, but mean people are…mean.

Leader: Correct.

Schooner: Mean people steal.

Leader: Right.

Schooner: They cheat.

Leader: That's true.

Schooner: …and they just might sneak up while I'm sleeping and pluck my tail feathers for a pillow! *Squawk!*

Leader: Now, now, Schooner.

Schooner: Or a pretty hat!

Leader: Calm down, Schooner.

Schooner: or…or…a feather bed! *(Schooner faints.)*

Leader: I'd never allow that to happen, Schooner.

Schooner: *(Schooner slowly revives)* Whew! Thanks, boss.

Leader: Jesus knows all about what people do. The nice ones and the mean ones.

Schooner: Can I peck the mean ones?

Leader: No.

Schooner:. *(sighs)* And Jesus loves the nice people the most, right?

Leader: No. Think about it. Jesus loves you and me, right?

Schooner: Of course! We're kind and helpful, and clever, and we're both totally nice.

Leader: But are we nice all the time? Never an eensy-weensy bit selfish or snotty?

Schooner: *(pauses)* Well, there was that one time…

Leader: Yes?

Schooner: I nibbled an entire bag of cheese crackers all by myself.

Leader: What did the other birds think?

Schooner: They said I was selfish. Wow, I'm sure glad Jesus loves me even when I blow it.

Leader: Jesus is always ready to forgive.

Schooner: And he'll forgive anybody?

Leader: You bet. The nice people…

Schooner: …the not-so-nice people.

Leader: The nice birds…

Schooner: …and those who are just a little cuckoo.

Leader: And because Jesus loves everyone, he can help you.

Schooner: …I can share my crackers with my friends—and with new friends!

Leader: Great job, Schooner! Let's head for the nearest fig tree for today's Bible story.

Schooner: A tree, huh?

Leader: We're off.

Schooner: Don't "leaf" without me!

Leader: Let's "leaf" together.

Schooner: That reminds me of an old saying Grandpa Bird was fond of…something about two birds in the bush…

Leader: …are better than two in a pillow!

Schooner: Ouch! I heard that.

Leader: Just a little joke between friends, Schooner.

Schooner: You just can't help yourself, can you?

Leader: Umm…Bible 4U! coming on through!

1 Bible 4U!

It's outrageous! I'm shocked. I'm speechless. (Well, almost.) I'm totally discombobulated, put out and perplexed. Why? Well, I'll tell you why.

You'd almost have to be from Jericho to understand, but I'll try to explain. There's this guy who is Mr. Awful, to put it kindly. Everybody, and I mean everybody, despises him. He is the lowest of the low, the number one guy you don't want to meet on the street. He works for the Romans. He's a Jew like the rest of the people here, but he works with the enemy. He collects taxes for them. And he charges a little extra and keeps it for himself. He cheats his own people to make himself rich and keep the Romans happy.

Instant Prep
Choose two kids to play Zacchaeus. Create an adorable mini person by positioning the shorter actor behind the taller one. Pull a big shirt over both kids. The arms of the person behind go through the arms of the shirt. The arms of the person in front slip into shoes resting on a tabletop. Lay the "Zach's New View" script on the table.

Talk about rich! He's got to be just about the richest guy in town. Jericho is a nice town here. Merchants do good business. Tourists spend lots of money. And Zacchaeus always gets his cut. Year after year he overcharges for taxes, and year after year he grows richer.

Now Jesus is coming to town, and guess who wants to see him. Zacchaeus. What a joke. Being the shortest guy in town, he's going to have trouble seeing over the crowd. And, believe me, no one's going to move aside and let him get in front. It will be very interesting to see happens.

for Overachievers
Choose two kids in your drama team to create a Bible time mini Zacchaeus. Position one behind the other as described above. Slip the arms of the rear actor into a robe. Put the hands of the forward actor into sandals resting on a table. Encourage the person behind to make gestures appropriate to the story. Let the rest of the team be the disapproving crowd.

Zach's New View
Based on Luke 19:2–10

The two actors assemble Zacchaeus in front of the kids.

So tell me—what's the first thing you notice about me. I'm short, right?

Pat yourself on the head.

Well, for your information, being short is the least of my worries. I'm a mean, dirty rotten cheat. I've been cheating for so long I don't think I can ever stop.

Cover face with hands.

I work for the Romans, which is enough to make everybody hate me. But the truth is a lot worse than that. When I collect taxes, I always make sure to collect a little bit too much. Sometimes I collect a lot too much. And where does the extra go? To my moneybags. I'm rich. Rich, rich, rich.

Rub hands together.

But that doesn't make me happy. I don't know anybody who's as miserable as I am. I don't have a single friend in this whole town. When I walk down the street, people move to the other side. I can feel their eyes boring into my back. I'm just the rottenest guy in town and it's never going to change. Nobody cares about me, and who could blame them?

Shrug with open palms.

I know there's no hope for me, but I've heard that a prophet named Jesus is coming to town. They say he's done amazing things—healed people, fed great crowds. I don't know if there's anything he can do for a guy with a rotten heart, but I'm going anyway. And I'd better hurry. If the rest of the people get there before I do, I don't have a chance of seeing him.

Feet run.

Oh, rats!

Tall kids from the group move in front of him.

Look at all those people lining the street. I'll never see Jesus! Wait a minute—there's a big tree up there. And it looks like a good climbing tree. Up, up and away!

Tall kids transform into branches of a tree. Zacchaeus's arms and legs make climbing motions.

This is much better. I can see everything, but nobody can see me. These leaves make great camouflage. Hey! Here comes Jesus now. He's coming…he's coming…he's coming straight toward me!

Cover mouth with hands.

Oh, no! What am I gonna do?

He says he wants to come to my house. MY HOUSE? Everybody is as shocked as I am. "You bet, Lord! I'd be glad to have you. Just let me climb down."

Arms and legs climb down. Shield eyes with hand and look around.

Man, everybody looks angry. They don't like it that Jesus is coming to my house. But, when Jesus looks at me, he doesn't see what a dirty rotten creep I

am. He sees right through to my heart. He knows that I'm hurting. He knows I really want to change. And when I see the love in his face, I really believe I can change. Jesus will help me change—I feel it already!

"Ladies and gentlemen, I have an announcement to make. Jesus is in my life and I'm a new man. You probably find that hard to believe. I don't blame you. But here's what I'm going to do. Every person I've cheated, I'll pay back four times over. I want to make things right."

Now Jesus is telling everyone that salvation has come to this house today. Woohoo!

Clap, then wave fist in the air.

That means he's forgiven me. I get a fresh, clean start. Wow—I didn't know this could happen. I can't tell you what a great feeling this is.

If Jesus can love me, maybe some of these other people can learn to love me too. I'd love to have a few friends. Someone who brings me soup when I'm sick. Someone who invites me over on holidays. Someone who gives me a hug when I'm feeling rotten. Do you think that could ever happen?

After today, I have to believe *anything* can happen. Maybe Jesus' love will fill the hearts of these people as it filled my heart.

Cross hands over heart.

Then they can learn to love me as he loves me. And maybe, just maybe, someone will be my friend. If I were in your town, would you be my friend?

I'll bet you know somebody who seems as mean and awful as I was. If Jesus could change me, he can change them. But who's going to show love to those people the way Jesus showed love to me? I guess that's up to YOU!

Point.

Wow—you talk about a big change in someone! Let's see how much of the Zacchaeus story you caught. Toss the four numbered balls to different parts of the room.

Bring the kids with the balls to the front one-by-one and ask these questions. Allow kids to get help from the group if they need it. After each correct answer, let kids drop the ball into a bag.

■ What did the people of Jericho think of Zacchaeus? Why?

■ Suppose you had been there when Jesus said to Zacchaeus, "I'm going to your house today." What would you have said to the friends around you?

■ If Zacchaeus had cheated you out of a lot of money, do you think you could forgive him? How would you do it?

■ How did Jesus make such a change in Zacchaeus's life?

We think about people in terms of the way they treat us. If they're mean or rude, we think, "Wow, that person's not very nice." But Jesus has a different way of thinking about people. He sees past what they do and right into their hearts.

When Jesus looked into Zacchaeus's heart, he saw hurt and sadness. And he knew his love could make a difference. When Zacchaeus looked at Jesus, he saw someone clean and pure and loving. Zacchaeus wanted to be like that. He wanted to get rid of all the ugliness and sin in his life and start fresh. Jesus gave him that chance.

Bible Verse
We love because he first loved us.
1 John 4:19

Jesus is willing to give everyone that chance. That's what Jesus is all about. No one else can take the bad stuff out of our lives. So what is *your* job? To show the kind of love that Jesus showed, even to people who are mean to you. Sound tough? It is! But today in your shepherd groups, you'll find out how to begin.

Dismiss kids to their shepherd groups.

Bible 4U!

2 Shepherd's Spot

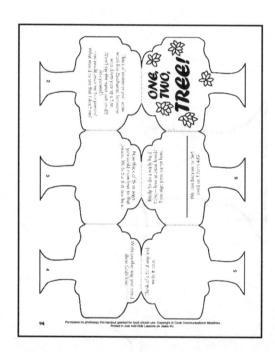

Gather your small group and help kids find Luke 19:2–10 in their Bibles.

Jesus made a habit of surprising people! Sometimes it was with a miracle, sometimes it was with the things he taught. But today's story was different. Jesus suddenly invited himself to the house of one of the worst guys in town. People couldn't believe their eyes! Let's read all about it.

Have volunteers take turns reading the Bible passage aloud.

■ **Who do you think was more surprised—Zacchaeus or the people in the crowd? What makes you think that?**

I'll bet you know somebody who reminds you of Zacchaeus. Jesus wants you to show his love to people like that. That's a lot to ask, isn't it? That's why we're going take it step by step.

Pass out scissors and copies of "One, Two, Tree!" Lead kids in these steps to assemble the tree booklet.

1. **Fold the sheet in half the long way.**
2. **Cut out the trees on the heavy lines. Be sure not to cut between the trees.**
3. **Fold the page in a Z shape to make a six-page booklet.**

Have get in pairs or trios to work through the questions in the booklet. As kids finish, bring them back into one group.

Signing this booklet is a big deal. It means that you're going to try to love as Jesus loves. Why should you do that? Let's read the Bible verse on page 6. Read, "We love because he first loved us."

■ **What does that mean to you?**

We don't deserve Jesus' love more than anyone else. We've all done bad things and we need Jesus to forgive us. Now Jesus expects us to pass that love onto others. Before you go, I'm going to pray that God will help you do that.

Let kids share prayer requests, then close with prayer. **Dear Jesus, you amazed everyone with your love for Zacchaeus. We need you to fill our hearts with that same love, so we can love unlovable people too. Today we pray for (mention kids' requests). Thank you for hearing our prayers, amen.**

One, Two, TREE!

Think of someone you know who's like Zacchaeus. Someone who drives you up a tree. (Don't say the name out loud!) Ask yourself: How would Jesus see this person? What would he see that I don't see?

Now think of three ways you could show love to that person. Write the first one here.

Ready to do a really hard thing—love as Jesus loved? Then sign your name here.

We love because he first loved us. 1 John 4:19

Write another way you could show God's love.

Think of a third way and write it here.

2

3

6

4

5

Workshop Wonders

Figs come in handy when you're short. Well, at least a fig tree did for Zacchaeus in today's story! Even though taxman Zacchaeus was not well liked, Jesus loved him. Why? Because Zacchaeus had faith in Jesus. He believed in him. Once a lost soul, Zacchaeus became a member of the family of believers. Let's remember that Jesus loves the good, the bad, the popular and the unpopular. What we think about people should not be our top priority. Jesus wants us to love them as he does.

Before we make our snack, let's learn some fun facts about figs!

- ■ First, let's all say "fun fig facts" three times fast!
- ■ Now take a guess. How many times is the word "fig" mentioned in the Bible? (Answer: 50 times.)

Good guessing! Sweet figs are known as one of the "blessing" foods found in the Holy Land.

- ■ Now for a little True or False! Jesus wouldn't think of going to the house of a dishonest tax collector. (False. Luke 19:5.)

- ■ True or False. Zaccheaus had a dirty house so he did not invite Jesus in. (False. Luke 19:6).
- ■ In Bible times the fig was a symbol of peace, riches and this three-letter word. Hint: the word rhymes with "toy." (Answer: joy!)

What fun! Christ's love and joy make a delicious combination. Let's make a fig tree snack to celebrate the love we read about in today's Bible story.

In a large mixing cup, mix 8-ounces of cream cheese with 1 cup of shredded carrots and 1/2 cup of chopped figs, 2 Tbsp. of honey and 1/2 tsp. of ground cinnamon (enough for about eight kids). Distribute the soft tortillas. Ask kids to spread the mixture out to the edges of the tortillas and roll them up. Cut the treat in half. **Spread extra cream cheese on the bottom of your plate and stand up your tortilla rolls to form two small sycamore-fig trees like the one mentioned in today's story.**

- ■ We love because Jesus first loved us. Name all the people who have taken care of you since you were a baby. How does this help you to treat others with love?
- ■ Would friends make fun of you if you sat next to the unpopular kid at lunch? Why does Jesus want us to do it anyway?

Have students insert tender celery "branches" into the top of each "tree." Sprinkle extra cinnamon on the bottom of their plates for a soil or ground-like effect. If you brought gummy figures to class have kids place a small Zacchaeus in the branches of their snacks.

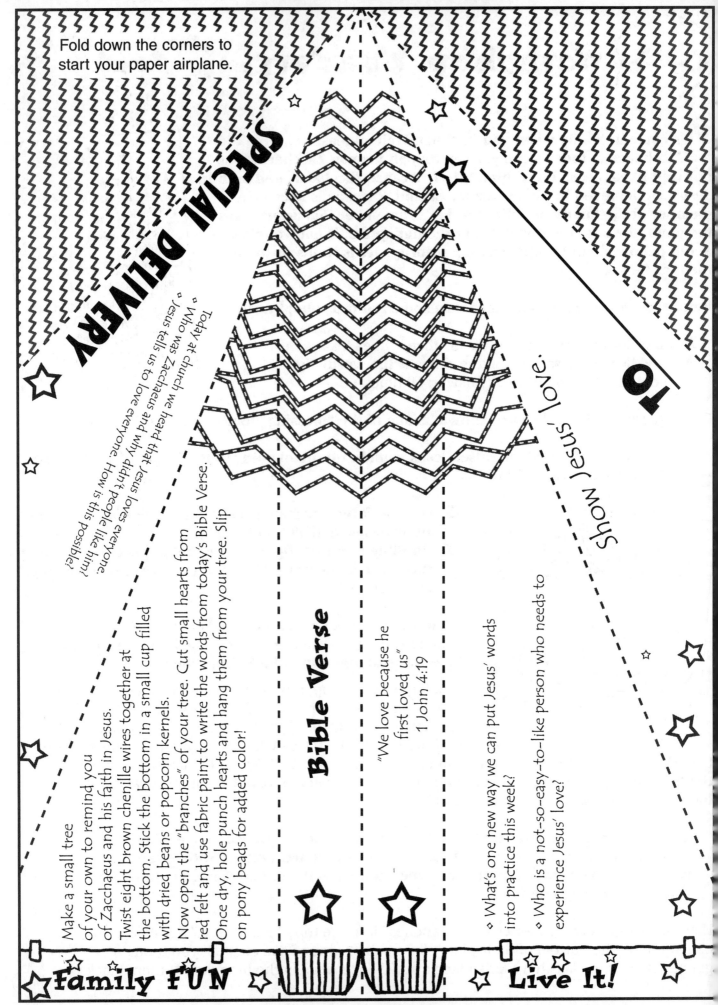

Fold down the corners to start your paper airplane.

SPECIAL DELIVERY

TO

Show Jesus' love.

Today at church we heard that Jesus loves everyone and why didn't people like him? "Who was Zacchaeus?" Jesus tells us to love everyone. How is this possible!

Bible Verse

"We love because he first loved us"
1 John 4:19

Make a small tree of your own to remind you of Zacchaeus and his faith in Jesus. Twist eight brown chenille wires together at the bottom. Stick the bottom in a small cup filled with dried beans or popcorn kernels. Now open the "branches" of your tree. Cut small hearts from red felt and use fabric paint to write the words from today's Bible Verse. Once dry, hole punch hearts and hang them from your tree. Slip on pony beads for added color!

◊ What's one new way we can put Jesus' words into practice this week?

◊ Who is a not-so-easy-to-like person who needs to experience Jesus' love?

Family FUN

Live It!

Through the Roof

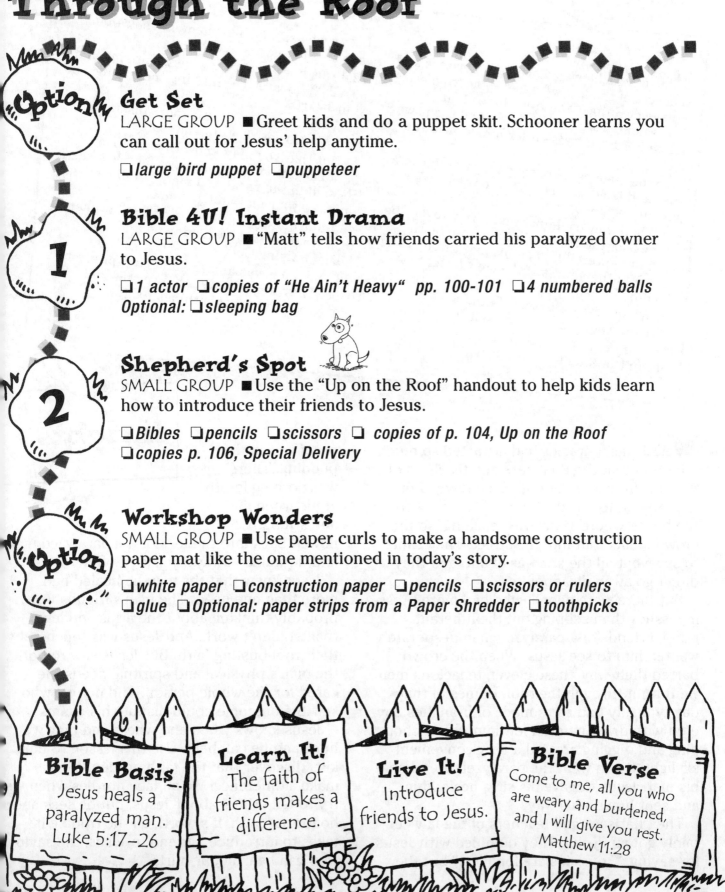

Get Set
LARGE GROUP ■ Greet kids and do a puppet skit. Schooner learns you can call out for Jesus' help anytime.

❏ large bird puppet ❏ puppeteer

1 Bible 4U! Instant Drama
LARGE GROUP ■ "Matt" tells how friends carried his paralyzed owner to Jesus.

❏ 1 actor ❏ copies of "He Ain't Heavy" pp. 100-101 ❏ 4 numbered balls
Optional: ❏ sleeping bag

2 Shepherd's Spot
SMALL GROUP ■ Use the "Up on the Roof" handout to help kids learn how to introduce their friends to Jesus.

❏ Bibles ❏ pencils ❏ scissors ❏ copies of p. 104, Up on the Roof
❏ copies p. 106, Special Delivery

Workshop Wonders
SMALL GROUP ■ Use paper curls to make a handsome construction paper mat like the one mentioned in today's story.

❏ white paper ❏ construction paper ❏ pencils ❏ scissors or rulers
❏ glue ❏ Optional: paper strips from a Paper Shredder ❏ toothpicks

Bible Basis
Jesus heals a paralyzed man.
Luke 5:17–26

Learn It!
The faith of friends makes a difference.

Live It!
Introduce friends to Jesus.

Bible Verse
Come to me, all you who are weary and burdened, and I will give you rest.
Matthew 11:28

Quick Takes

Luke 5:17–26

One day as he was teaching, Pharisees and teachers of the law, who had come from every village of Galilee and from Judea and Jerusalem, were sitting there. And the power of the Lord was present for him to heal the sick.

18 Some men came carrying a paralytic on a mat and tried to take him into the house to lay him before Jesus.

19 When they could not find a way to do this because of the crowd, they went up on the roof and lowered him on his mat through the tiles into the middle of the crowd, right in front of Jesus.

20 When Jesus saw their faith, he said, "Friend, your sins are forgiven."

21 The Pharisees and the teachers of the law began thinking to themselves, "Who is this fellow who speaks blasphemy? Who can forgive sins but God alone?"

22 Jesus knew what they were thinking and asked, "Why are you thinking these things in your hearts?

23 Which is easier: to say, 'Your sins are forgiven,' or to say, 'Get up and walk'?

24 But that you may know that the Son of Man has authority on earth to forgive sins...." He said to the paralyzed man, "I tell you, get up, take your mat and go home."

25 Immediately he stood up in front of them, took what he had been lying on and went home praising God.

26 Everyone was amazed and gave praise to God. They were filled with awe and said, "We have seen remarkable things today."

Insights

Well! Jesus' miracles had attracted so much attention that the Pharisees and teachers of the Law from all over Galilee converged on Capernaum to check him out. They packed the house where Jesus was teaching, so the crowd spilled out into the street. They came to see what all the stir was about, and they didn't go away disappointed.

But there were people who had more pressing issues than scoping out the itinerant rabbi. Friends of a paralyzed man desperately wanted him to see Jesus. When the crowd barred their way, these clever, tenacious men went right through the roof. Homes of that day typically had roofs made of branches covered with dried mud. A few minutes of chopping and digging created a very convenient skylight! Down went the paralyzed friend on his mat. Jesus forgave his sins, healed him, and sent him on his way.

The Pharisees and teachers of the law certainly got an eyeful. They quibbled with Jesus for saying, "Your sins are forgiven," but the proof was in the pudding. There was nothing left to argue when life and strength flowed back into the legs of the paralyzed man and he walked away, praising God.

Jesus knew that the man he healed had more than one need. The man's friends were probably thinking about the arms and legs that wouldn't work. And Jesus was touched by their roof-busting faith. But Jesus saw to both the man's physical and spiritual needs. He cared for the whole person. And no one who saw the outcome could dispute his claims.

Jesus knows when and where and how we hurt, and he can help. Use this lesson to help kids discover that the faith of friends can make a difference! We all face hurdles when we try to tell others about Jesus, but he sees and honor our faith. It's worth all the trouble it takes to introduce a friend to Jesus, the savior who can heal all our hurts.

Option Get Set

Hello everyone. Thanks for dropping by today. It's nice to have friends, isn't it? Friends make all the difference—in good times and when we just can't go it alone. Schooner, come up here and see all our friends. *Schooner pops up.*

Schooner: Hi, boss. Did you say something about friends? Oh, man—I really need a friend.

Leader: What's the matter?

Schooner: It's my Aunt Squawk. She's down with a sprained wing. I should say, she's up with a sprained wing.

Leader: Huh?

Schooner: Well, since she hurt her wing she can't fly. So she's stuck up in her tree.

Leader: That's awful. Is there anything I can do to help?

Schooner: Yes. I promised to take her dinner.

Leader: That was nice of you.

Schooner: There's just one little problem. She wants pancakes. But I don't know how to make them.

Leader: I can give you a hand with that. I'm one of the greatest pancake flippers of all time.

Schooner: Really?

Leader: Absolutely. What kind would you like to make? Blueberry, banana nut, chocolate chip, or walnut raisin?

Schooner: Birdseed

Leader: Birdseed?

Schooner: Yep. Aunt Squawk wants birdseed pancakes.

Leader: Sounds crunchy. All those seeds might get stuck in her teeth.

Schooner: Beak, boss. You have teeth, parrots have beaks. Nice sharp beaks. And we can bite too. Wanna' see?

Leader: Hey! What kind of talk is that? I haven't even made any chicken jokes today.

Schooner: Oops. I'm sorry. Will you still help me make pancakes?

Leader: Of course I will. Right after church. Right now we have all these kids who want to hear about Jesus.

Schooner: Jesus was good at helping people.

Leader: He was. But some people had a hard time getting to him.

Schooner: Like my Auntie Squawk? She can't go anywhere until her wing gets better. She'd be up a tree if I didn't help. I mean…she is up a tree, but…

Leader: I understand, Schooner. Today's Bible story is about someone who couldn't go anywhere either.

Schooner: Did someone bring him birdseed pancakes?

Leader: They did better than that. They brought him to Jesus!

Schooner: Wowsers. I could never carry Aunt Squawk. She's got a little too much, um, wingspan.

Leader: You don't need to feel bad about that. It took four friends to bring this man to Jesus.

Schooner: How did they do it?

Leader: They went through the roof.

Schooner: My dad went through the roof once when I stepped on his reading glasses.

Leader: There's more than one way to go through the roof.

Schooner: You mean going through the roof can be a good thing?

Leader: It sure can. I'd say you have something to learn from today's Bible story.

Schooner: Well, don't keep me in suspense!

Leader: I wouldn't think of it. Are you ready, everyone? Here comes Bible 4U!

1 Bible 4U!

It's another busy day in Capernaum. That little fishing village was Jesus' home away from home. Lots of his friends lived there. Jesus had been traveling around to different towns, teaching and preaching and healing people. Now that he was back in Capernaum, everyone wanted to see him.

In fact, the house where he was staying was so crowded that there were people spilling out into the street. Not one more person could squish inside.

Instant Prep

Before class, ask a talented, outgoing reader to play the role of Matt. Give him a copy of "He Ain't Heavy" to review. Or, play Matt yourself. If you have a blanket handy, wind it around your feet and stand in place as you tell the story.

That was a problem for four men who'd brought their friend to see Jesus. The friend was paralyzed: he couldn't move his arms or his legs. The four men knew Jesus could heal him. But how could they get the man to Jesus? All those people were in the way.

As you'll find out, getting their friend to Jesus was so important that they weren't about to let a crowd get in their way. It didn't take long for them to come up with Plan B. But I don't want to give away the whole story. Let's welcome our friend Matt!

for Overachievers

Choose an actor with a good solid funny bone to prepare this story. "Dress" him in a lightweight sleeping bag that comes all the way up to chest level. Have him make his entrance and exit by bouncing across the stage.

He Ain't Heavy
Based on Luke 5:17–26

Hi there. I'm Matt. Matt rhymes with flat. And I just happen to be a flat mat. You'd be flat too if someone had lain on you for years and years. But now, for the first time ever, I'm going to have a chance to get fluffy. Fluffy, puffy, no longer a toughie! Oh yeah, baby.

I'm going to get shaken out, washed in the lake, and hung up to dry in the sun. I'm going to stretch, flap a little in the breeze, and take in a few rays. I just can't wait! So why is everything changing? Jesus did it!

Until today my owner has been paralyzed. His arms and legs wouldn't work. I felt bad for him. He couldn't do anything but lie around all day—on me! That's how I got to be such a flat mat. Day in and day out my owner would lie on me. I didn't get a break like most sleeping mats. They get used a few hours each night, then they get a shake and roll up until the next night. I had no such luck. It's been months since I had a cleaning.

Sniff your shoulder.

Yuck. I can't stand not being fresh. My life-changing adventure started this morning. My owner was just lying around, like always, when four of his friends came up.

"Jesus is in town!" one of them said. "He's healed so many—surely he can heal you."

The next thing I knew I was being lifted by all four corners. They carried me across town. When we got to the house where Jesus was teaching, I thought my adventure was just about over. But, no! It was just beginning. The house was full of people. There was no way we could get inside. It looked hopeless.

But my owner's friends weren't about to give up. They picked up my four corners again and headed for the stairs to the roof. I have never done stairs before. They had to hold up one end of me so my owner didn't tumble off and roll down. When we got to the roof I thought, "What in the world are we doing here?" Jesus was inside—straight underneath us.

Then the friends started whacking the roof with sticks and digging pieces of it away. The people in the house must have freaked out when branches and dried mud started falling on them. It didn't take long for them to make a good sized hole. Then they lifted my corners and dangled my owner and me over the hole. It was terrifying! What if they dropped us? It was awful! I couldn't look.

Shake and cover your eyes.

But they were careful. Inch by inch they lowered us until we found ourselves right in front of Jesus. I have never seen a kinder face. (Of course, it's not faces I usually see.) He spoke to my owner. "Son," he said. "Your sins are forgiven." Some people in the room got all hot and bothered over that. They thought Jesus was an ordinary man who didn't have the right to forgive sins. But they were wrong.

Jesus turned back to my owner and said, "Rise, pick up your mat and walk." Did you hear that? Jesus mentioned me! Pretty cool, huh?

You could hear a gasp go all around the room. My master leaned forward and put weight on his legs. They held! He pushed off the ground with his arms. They worked! Then, surely and steadily, he rose to he feet. His smile was so big it looked like it would split his face! Then my owner rolled me up.

Spin.

Do you know how dizzy that makes me? Round and round until I'm all folded into a neat little bundle. My owner threw me over his shoulder, and off we went, praising God.

All these years I had carried him. Now he was carrying me. You talk about a wonderful feeling! The crowd parted as we went through. People whispered, "How did Jesus do that? He must be the Son of God!"

You know, those four friends made all the difference. Without them, my owner and I would never have gotten to Jesus. Maybe you know somebody who needs to find Jesus. What could you do to help them?

Aaaaa!

Act as if you're being pulled away.

I think it's laundry time.

Wave and exit.

Bible 4U!

Matt was a pretty nice guy, huh? Not to mention the four friends who brought the paralyzed man to Jesus. Let me toss out a few questions about today's Bible story.

Toss the four numbered balls to different parts of the room. Bring the kids with the balls to the front one-by-one and ask these questions. Allow kids to get help from the group if they need it. After each correct answer, let kids drop the ball into a bag.

 ■ What was life like for the paralyzed man before he met Jesus?

 ■ If you had been in the house where Jesus was teaching, what would you have thought when the hole in the roof started growing?

 ■ What did Jesus say that surprised many people?

 ■ What would you be willing to do to bring a friend to Jesus?

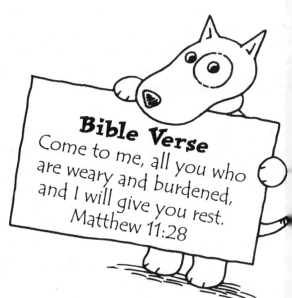

Bible Verse
Come to me, all you who are weary and burdened, and I will give you rest. Matthew 11:28

There are lots of people who need a healing touch from Jesus. Some of them have hurt bodies, like the man in today's story. But lots of them have hearts that are hurting. Maybe it's because their family broke up. Maybe a pet died. Maybe they just don't have anyone to be a friend.

Jesus cares about all those hurts. And he can help. But you need to help too. Like the men in today's story, you can be the friends who bring hurting people to Jesus.

People can't come to Jesus for help unless they know about him. They need to know that he is the Son of God and that he came to earth to show us how to live. People need to know that Jesus lived as a man, and he understands what it's like to hurt. And they need to know that his loving touch on their lives can bring comfort and help. You have lots of good news to share!

There's no time to waste. Let's get right to our shepherd groups and learn how we can introduce our friends to Jesus!

Dismiss the kids to their small groups.

2 Shepherd's Spot

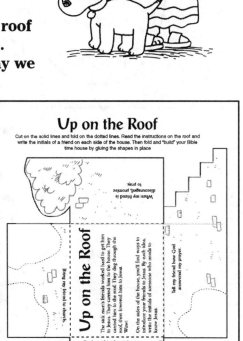

Gather your small group and help kids find Luke 5 in their Bibles.

Wow! The four friends in today's Bible story really raised the roof, didn't they? The roofs in Jesus' time weren't like the roofs we have on our houses today. They were flat roofs made of dried mud laid over branches. And there were stairs going up the outside of the house.

When the day had been hot, families enjoyed going up on the roof to enjoy the cool evening air. Sometimes they even slept there. Houses weren't very big, so they used the roof in the same way we use decks today.

Let's read the story from the Bible and see what happened on this particular roof. Have volunteers read Luke 5:17–26 aloud.

These men wanted to get their friend to Jesus, and they wouldn't let anything stop them. I had a friend like that. Share a personal experience of someone who helped you find healing in Jesus during a difficult time. Then invite kids to share their experience.

Do you think you can introduce your friends to Jesus? Well, you can! Here's how. Distribute the "Up on the Roof" handout. Ask volunteers to read the ideas on each side of the house.

■ **Whose initials can you put by each idea?**

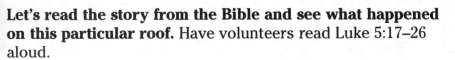

Encourage kids to think of friends and family member who need to hear about Jesus. Then help kids cut out the figure and form a 3D house by gluing the sides together.

See the message on the stairs? That's Jesus' invitation to everyone. Be sure to share it this week.

Ask kids to share their concerns, then close with prayer. **Dear Lord, it's so wonderful to know you. Your love touches all our hurts and brings us comfort. Today we pray for** (mention children's concerns). **Help us find ways to introduce people to you this week, amen.**

Up on the Roof

Cut on the solid lines and fold on the dotted lines. Read the instructions on the roof and write the initials of a friend on each side of the house. Then fold and "build" your Bible time house by gluing the shapes in place

When my friend is discouraged, promise to pray.

Bring my friend to church.

Up on the Roof

The sick man's friends worked hard to get him to Jesus. They carried him to the house. They dug through the roof, then lowered him to Jesus. Wow!

On the sides of the house, you'll find ways to introduce your friends to Jesus. By each idea, write the initials of someone who needs to know Jesus.

Tell my friend how God answered my prayer.

Teach my friend a cool song from church.

Workshop Wonders

Get List:
- ❏ white paper
- ❏ construction paper
- ❏ pencils
- ❏ scissors or rulers
- ❏ glue

Optional:
- ❏ Paper Shredder strips
- ❏ toothpicks

Pass out the plain white paper. **Today's Bible story talks of a paralyzed man and the mat that was his bed as well as his transportation. More than likely, this mat was a thin bedroll, like a lightweight sleeping bag that we might use today on a summer-night's campout or sleepover.**

Pass out the white paper. **I'd like you to make a pencil drawing on your paper of what the mat mentioned in today's Bible story might have looked like. For our purposes, think colorful: draw stripes, design patterns, color circles. Leave space at the bottom of the page for the Bible verse.**

Once you're done, we'll enhance it with quilled paper curls to make soft, comfy 3-D mat. It will be a colorful reminder that Jesus has our hurts "covered."

Let kids cut (or tear against a ruler's edge) colorful construction paper into strips about 1/2-inch wide. Show them how to make a small fold at one end of each strip and roll it up into a tight spiral. Younger children may want to roll the strips around a pencil.

■ **If you could spend a summer introducing Jesus to children in a foreign country, what country would you choose?**

Let the paper spirals relax a bit before gluing them flat side down on your paper. Follow your pencil drawing. Make sure to leave a bit of space between each paper curl but do try to fill in your entire "mat" with color.

■ **We know people sometimes hurt in their bodies. What other kinds of hurts can Jesus help with?**

Print today's Bible verse under your picture once you're done. Remember that in today's verse, the word rest means more than a good night's sleep. When we're hurting, Jesus words are a comforting ray of help and hope for body and spirit. Today's verse: "Come to me, all you who are weary and burdened, and I will give you rest" Matthew 11:28.

■ **What problems come to mind when you think of Jesus' words "weary and burdened?"**

■ **How is Jesus' love like a warm, comforting blanket?**

Your mats look beautiful! Let them remind you that Jesus' love brings help and comfort to hurting people.

Fold down the corners to start your paper airplane.

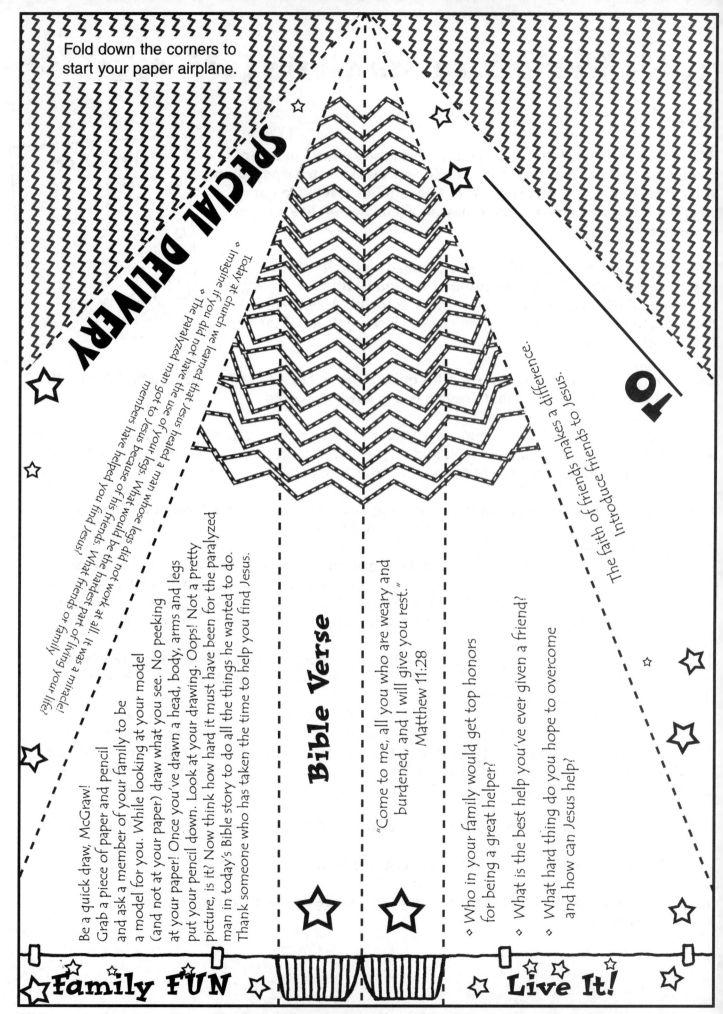

SPECIAL DELIVERY

TO

The faith of friends makes a difference.
Introduce friends to Jesus.

Today at church we learned that Jesus healed a man whose legs did not work at all. It was a miracle! "Imagine if you did not have the use of your legs. What would be the hardest part of living your life?" "The paralyzed man got to Jesus because of his friends. What friends or family members have helped you find Jesus?"

Be a quick draw, McGraw! Grab a piece of paper and pencil and ask a member of your family to be a model for you. While looking at your model (and not at your paper) draw what you see. No peeking at your paper! Once you've drawn a head, body, arms and legs put your pencil down. Look at your drawing. Oops! Not a pretty picture, is it? Now think how hard it must have been for the paralyzed man in today's Bible story to do all the things he wanted to do. Thank someone who has taken the time to help you find Jesus.

Bible Verse

"Come to me, all you who are weary and burdened, and I will give you rest." Matthew 11:28

◇ Who in your family would get top honors for being a great helper?

◇ What is the best help you've ever been given a friend?

◇ What hard thing do you hope to overcome and how can Jesus help?

Family FUN

Live It!

One Sword Too Many

Option

Get Set
LARGE GROUP ■ Greet kids and do a puppet skit. Schooner learns about trusting God and being part of his plan.

❑ large bird puppet ❑ puppeteer

1

Bible 4U! Instant Drama
LARGE GROUP ■ Peter and John discuss what happened when soldiers arrested Jesus.

❑ 2 actors ❑ copies of pp. 110-110 Peter and John script ❑ 4 numbered balls Optional: ❑ 2 Bibletime costumes ❑ plastic sword

2

Shepherd's Spot
SMALL GROUP ■ Use the "Trust Balloon" handout as a reminder to trust Jesus when everything goes wrong.

❑ Bibles ❑ pencils ❑ scissors ❑ copies of p. 114, Trust Balloon
❑ copies p. 116, Special Delivery

Option

Workshop Wonders
SMALL GROUP ■ Become an olive tree in the middle of a garden to reinforce today's Bible verse.

❑ green or purple balloons ❑ dry rice ❑ funnels ❑ index cards ❑ scissors
❑ hole punch ❑ pencils/markers ❑ music CD and CD player

Bible Basis
Peter defends Jesus. John 18:1–11

Learn It!
Jesus knows what's best.

Live It!
Trust in God's plan.

Bible Verse
Even though I walk through the valley of the shadow of death, I will fear no evil, for you are with me; your rod and your staff, they comfort me. Psalm 23:4

Quick Takes

John 18:1–11

When he had finished praying, Jesus left with his disciples and crossed the Kidron Valley. On the other side there was an olive grove, and he and his disciples went into it.

2 Now Judas, who betrayed him, knew the place, because Jesus had often met there with his disciples.

3 So Judas came to the grove, guiding a detachment of soldiers and some officials from the chief priests and Pharisees. They were carrying torches, lanterns and weapons.

4 Jesus, knowing all that was going to happen to him, went out and asked them, "Who is it you want?"

5 "Jesus of Nazareth," they replied. "I am he," Jesus said. (And Judas the traitor was standing there with them.)

6 When Jesus said, "I am he," they drew back and fell to the ground.

7 Again he asked them, "Who is it you want?" And they said, "Jesus of Nazareth."

8 "I told you that I am he," Jesus answered. "If you are looking for me, then let these men go."

9 This happened so that the words he had spoken would be fulfilled: "I have not lost one of those you gave me."

10 Then Simon Peter, who had a sword, drew it and struck the high priest's servant, cutting off his right ear. (The servant's name was Malchus.)

11 Jesus commanded Peter, "Put your sword away! Shall I not drink the cup the Father has given me?"

Insights

The disciples didn't know what to do with Jesus' words and actions of late. On this night in Jerusalem he had taken on an especially somber note. As they ate, he'd spoken of giving his body and his blood. He said one of their close group would betray him, and Judas left. He prayed for them as if he'd no longer be with them.

These tired, confused disciples. Though they'd spent nearly three years with Jesus, this somber man was a stranger to them. They had come to Jerusalem at Passover, the perfect time to declare his lordship. It started off well enough, with crowds lining the streets crying, "Blessed is he who comes in the name of the Lord!" But the mood in the city quickly turned ugly—the work of the priests and teachers of the law, no doubt.

But Jesus could handle them. They'd never been able to top him in an argument. They'd never stopped a storm, fed a crowd of thousands from a small boy's lunch, or raised the dead. There was nothing to fear—was there? If they could get a little sleep, things would seem better in the morning.

But long before morning, Judas came to their quiet olive grove leading a detachment of soldiers. Would Jesus do nothing—he who held the power of God in his hands? The unthinkable was happening. Jesus was going to allow himself to be arrested like an ordinary criminal. Peter grabbed his sword and swung it at the high priest's servant. In the midst of this terrifying situation, he would strike at least one blow in defense of his Lord. But Jesus rebuked him and the bloody sword went back into its sheath.

When kids see an injustice going down, their instinct, like Peter's, is to do defend. And when they witness an unstoppable tragedy, it turns their sense of justice upside down. Isn't our loving God supposed to rule everything? How could this happen?

The walk of faith, has its darkest moments. Moments when we cry out, "No! It can't be! Somebody's got to stop this!" Use this lesson to help kids understand that the moments when good triumphs sometimes come not in this life, but the next. Our omnipotent God does allow appalling tragedies that rock our world. He, however, will write the final chapter, the chapter that we can't see, but only imagine. This lesson can encourage kids to move ahead with God even when the unthinkable happens. He has plan—never fear—a plan that will bring the greatest good out of the greatest tragedy.

Option Get Set

Greet your kids. **Hello! It's always a special time when we can come together and learn more about Jesus. We have lots to learn too—about trusting God and being part of his plan. Jesus did! And I know just the bird to help us out. Schooner, are you there?** *Schooner pops up.*

Schooner: Grrrrr…

Leader: What's up, Schooner? You seem angry.

Schooner: You got it, boss.

Leader: What's the problem?

Schooner: It's my best friend.

Leader: Yes…

Schooner: My best friend and I argue all the time.

Leader: Let's see if I can help. Why don't I play the part of your best friend?

Schooner: Fine! All you'll need to say is two words.

Leader: …which are?

Schooner: Do not!

Leader: I got it.

Schooner: *(speaks in an animated voice)* Hi, Jack. I know just the thing to serve at tonight's Creative Seed party.

Leader: Do not!

Schooner: Do too! I whipped up a delicious olive-and-cheese spread and a bowl of fruit nectar punch—with orange slices! I know what birds like.

Leader: Do not!

Schooner: Do too! I've scrubbed all the perches in my house and arranged to have the neighbor's cat far, far away. I know all about cats.

Leader: Do not!

Schooner: Do too! Hey, this is my party. I planned it and we're going to do it my way. I know what's best.

Leader: Do not!

Schooner: Do too!

Leader: Do not!

Schooner: Grrrrr….

Leader: I see the problem, Schooner.

Schooner: Yea, my best friend is a dodo bird!

Leader: No name calling, Schooner.

Schooner: *(under his breath)* Sorry.

Leader: The problem is you think you know what's best. And your friend thinks he knows too.

Schooner: It's my way or the highway! That's how I see it.

Leader: Hmm…

Schooner: Hit the road, Jack!

Leader: No wonder you've got problems, Schooner.

Schooner: But I know what's best. *I know, I know, I know!*

Leader: Not much room in all that "knowing" for a friendship, is there?

Schooner: *(sigh)*

Leader: When we follow God, we know that his way is best, his plans perfect.

Schooner: That much I know. God is wonderful.

Leader: And when Jesus, God's only Son, came to earth he needed to do his Father's will as well.

Schooner: *(shakes head)* I don't get that part, boss. Jesus was the Son of God. I bet he already knew what was best for him.

Leader: Jesus came to earth to save the world from sin…

Schooner: Yes…

Leader: …and to obey his Father's will.

Schooner: What about when things went wrong?

Leader: Even then Jesus trusted his Father.

Schooner: Because Jesus' Father knows best.

Leader: You got it! So let's be part of God's plan. He wants us to trust him no matter what happens.

Schooner: I'll give it a bird's-eye-try, boss!

Leader: Good for you, Schooner.

Leader and Schooner: Bible 4U! up next!

1 Bible 4U!

It was a dark and stormy night. Well, I don't know if was stormy, but it was dark! Jesus and his disciples ate supper together, then went outside and hiked across a valley to an olive grove. It was one of Jesus' favorite places. He often took the disciples there for quiet times.

Think about what it would be like to be there. Friendly, old olive trees surround you on the hillside. A cool night breeze stirs the leaves. It's been a long day and you're tired, glad to go to a familiar, restful place.

Instant Prep
Before class, ask two volunteers who are good readers to play the roles of Peter and John. Give them copies of the "Peter and John" script below. Encourage them to create an atmosphere of tension.

Suddenly torches light up the night. Soldiers and officials burst onto the scene and demand to know which person is Jesus. Judas points him out, then the soldiers tie him up. Peter's sword flashes in the torchlight. He strikes the ear of the high priest's servant. The soldiers step forward— anything could happen! Jesus tells Peter to put his sword away. Then the soldiers take Jesus away. They disappear over the hillside and the disciples are left alone in the garden once more.

Peter puts his sword down, then looks around and sees his good friend John.

for Overachievers
Have two members of your drama team prepare the roles of Peter and John. Create a darkened garden setting with a few backdrops that suggest an olive grove.

Peter and John
Based on John 18:1–11

Peter and John enter nervously, looking around to see if they're being followed.

Peter: John! I can't believe what just happened. This isn't how it was supposed to turn out!

John: I know, Peter. It's awful. They've taken our Lord away.

Peter: Why didn't Jesus let us try to stop them? Why didn't HE stop them?

John: I couldn't believe he let the soldiers tie him up and lead him away. He's not a criminal—he's the Son of God!

Peter: Do you remember how this week started? All the people were waving palms and shouting "Hosanna!" when he rode into the city.

John: That was just a few days ago. Now it seems like everyone has turned against him.

Peter: Even Judas. How could he have betrayed Jesus like that? He led them right to this spot.

John: I'm sure the high priest is behind this. He must have paid Judas to bring them here.

Peter: Things like this shouldn't happen. It's just not right.

John: How can they accuse Jesus of doing anything wrong? Who knows what they'll do to him now?

Peter: Should we get some people together and try to free him? He has thousands of followers in this city.

John: That's not what he wants, Peter. You heard what he said.

Peter: Yeah. "Put your sword away! Shall I not drink the cup the Father has given me?"

John: You tried to protect him, Peter. I mean, one minute it was all quiet and dark here in the olive grove. Then all of sudden the officials and soldiers came with torches and weapons.

Peter: I couldn't stand it when they put their hands on Jesus. That's why I slashed at that man with my sword.

John: You know what? We have to believe that God is going to bring good from this.

Peter: How can anything good come out of Jesus, being arrested? And what are we supposed to do now? Go after him? Hide? Head for the hills?

John: Those are all good questions. The only answer I have is to trust God.

Peter: I wish I could. I wish I could just believe that he is going to make everything turn out okay.

John: Do you remember what Jesus told us earlier this evening? He said, "do not let your hearts be troubled. Trust in God; trust also in me."

Peter: Trust. How are we supposed to trust? Our world is falling apart.

John: He talked about heaven, too. Remember?

Peter: Yeah, but I didn't get it. He said something about going to prepare a place for us in his Father's house.

John: Right. That means heaven. And he promised to come back for us and take us to be with him there.

Peter: What does he mean when he talks about going away? You don't think…I mean, they're not going to…

John: I don't know what will happen anymore than you do. But Jesus talked a lot about doing the will of his Father. This must be part of God's plan. We don't know what's going to happen, but God does.

Peter: It seems like everything is going wrong.

John: I know. The thing is, we don't know the whole picture. But think of all the times Jesus has turned something bad into something good. He calmed the storm, healed diseases, even raised people from the dead. Even now, he can make something good happen.

Peter: So you think we're just supposed to hang on.

John: Right. And keep praying and trusting God.

Peter: And believe that he'll make something good happen from all this?

John: Exactly.

Peter: But, John, I thought Jesus was going to be king!

John: He is king, Peter. King of the whole world. And king of our hearts. He wouldn't be in the hands of his enemies right now unless he was willing to be.

Peter: That's true. I'll keep trusting God. At least I'll try.

John: Good.

Peter: Do you think it would be okay if I followed at a distance to see where they took him?

John: I think it would be fine. Be careful, though.

Peter: Okay—I'm outta here. What are you going to do?

John: I'm going to pray. Watch your back, brother.

Peter: You too.

They exit in opposite directions.

Bible 4U!

Peter and John could hardly believe what they had just seen. Jesus, who had done miracle after miracle, just stood there and let soldiers arrest him. The man they had followed for three years was gone. They didn't know what would happen next. Let's see how well you caught the story.

Toss the four numbered balls to different parts of the room. Bring the kids with the balls to the front one-by-one and ask these questions. Allow kids to get help from the group if they need it. After each correct answer, let kids drop the ball into a bag.

 ■ Explain who came to arrest Jesus and why they wanted to take him away.

 ■ Why did Jesus let the soldiers arrest him? Why didn't he do a miracle to stop them?

 ■ If you had been one of the disciples, what would you have done when the soldiers took Jesus away?

 ■ How could the disciples have helped each other at this difficult time?

Bible Verse
Even though I walk through the valley of the shadow of death, I will fear no evil, for you are with me; your rod and your staff, they comfort me.
Psalm 23:4

Life is full of surprises—some good ones and some bad ones. We just never know what a day might bring. When Jesus' disciples sat with him at supper that night, they had no idea what was in store.

There's one important thing I want you to remember. Ready? God is never surprised. He knows all about our lives. He's there to help us through hard times. His Word encourages us and tells us over and over to trust in him.

God wants us to turn to him for comfort. Think of praying like this: "God, we don't understand what's happening. Please protect us and help us to see you are near."

Imagine yourself crawling into God's lap and snuggling into his arms. The Bible teaches us that we can call God "Daddy." Isn't that awesome? We don't understand everything that happens, but we do know that we can trust God's promises to watch over us.

Today in your shepherd groups you'll learn how to remind each other to trust God when it seems like everything is going wrong.

Dismiss kids to their shepherd groups.

② Shepherd's Spot

Gather your small group and help kids find John 18 in their Bibles.

In today's story, Jesus' disciples were surprised and scared out of their wits. It had only been four days since Palm Sunday when everyone cheered Jesus and welcomed him to town. But things changed very quickly.

Have volunteers take turns reading John 18:1–11 aloud.

■ **Did you ever find yourself shocked and surprised when something bad happened? What was that like?**

When things like this happen, and you have that terrible feeling in your stomach, remember that God knows how things will turn out, and he is at work.

Distribute the "Trust Balloons" handout and lead kids through the assembly. Fold the page in half and cut out the figure on the heavy lines. Fold the flaps at the bottom forward to make a stand. You may want to let kids add bright colors to the balloon.

Ask a volunteer to read the Bible verse on the base of the card.

■ **What does this verse promise? How do the words encourage you to hang in there?**

Put your Trust Balloon in a spot where it can remind you that no matter what happens, God is at work and he will take care of you. His love will lift you and carry you through troubled clouds

Before you close with prayer, invite kids to share their concerns. **Dear Heavenly Father, it's so good to know that there are no surprises to you. Thank you for inviting us to call you "Daddy" and letting us turn to you for comfort. Help us remember, no matter what happens, that we can trust in you. Right now we pray for** (mention each child's requests). **We praise you with all our hearts. In Jesus' name, amen.**

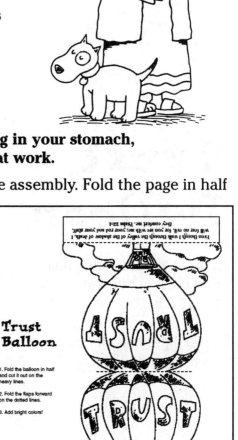

Trust Balloon

1. Fold the balloon in half and cut it out on the heavy lines.

2. Fold the flaps forward on the dotted lines.

3. Add bright colors!

Even though I walk through the valley of the shadow of death, I will fear no evil, for you are with me; your rod and your staff, they comfort me. Psalm 23:4

Even though I walk through the valley of the shadow of death, I will fear no evil, for you are with me; your rod and your staff, they comfort me. Psalm 23:4

Trust Balloon

1. Fold the balloon in half and cut it out on the heavy lines.

2. Fold the flaps forward on the dotted lines.

3. Add bright colors!

Even though I walk through the valley of the shadow of death, I will fear no evil, for you are with me; your rod and your staff, they comfort me. Psalm 23:4

Workshop Wonders

How would you feel if you turned the corner and saw a big kid pushing your little brother off his bike? What if you got there just in time to see the bully speeding off and your brother on the ground crying?

■ Has something like this ever happened to you? How did it make you feel? What did you do or want to do?

That's how Peter felt that night in the olive grove. Everything was dark and quiet. Then suddenly blazing torches lit up the night as soldiers came to take Jesus away. Peter raised his sword to defend his teacher and friend, but Jesus told him to put the sword down. Jesus knew this was part of God's plan.

Get List:
❑ green or purple balloons
❑ dry rice
❑ funnels
❑ index cards
❑ pencils

Let's remember the experience of that night with an Olive Tree Challenge. First we need to make olives! Set out balloons, funnels, measuring cups and rice. Place the balloon opening over the narrow end of the funnel. Pour in 1/4 cup of rice. Without sucking in any of the rice, blow up the balloon about half full and tie off.

Isn't this a lovely olive? Now each of you can make one. Beware: Consider the age of your class before assigning this activity. Avoid any choking hazard (both mouth and nose) and choose to make filled balloons before class and have them ready for use. **Now for the stem.** Use a pencil to poke a hole through the center of an index card. Push the end of the balloon through the hole. Help kids do the same.

Now you get to be the branch. Balance your olive on one shoulder. Hold out your arms and sway in the breeze, but don't let your olive fall off! Let kids practice moving with their olives balanced on their shoulders.

Find two other "branches" and make a "tree" by touching fingertips in the center of a circle. Help kids form trees. You may need to have one or two trees with four branches.

Now a gentle wind is blowing through the grove. Rotate slowly, but don't let your olives fall off. If someone's olive falls off, your tree becomes a "bush" and kneels (or sits) **down until the next round begins.**

The breeze is picking up. Go a little faster! Let kids keep going for a few seconds.

Oh, no! The soldiers are coming with burning torches. You don't want your olives to get burned. Turn faster! Keeping picking up the pace until all the trees have been eliminated. Then scramble the branches to form new trees and play again.

After several rounds, try a relay game. Then gather kids in a circle. **When soldiers arrested Jesus, Peter thought it was the most awful thing in the world. But Jesus knew that God would bring something good from the terrible things that were about to happen. When bad things happen, keep trusting God. He has a plan and he promises to watch over you.**

Fold down the corners to start your paper airplane.

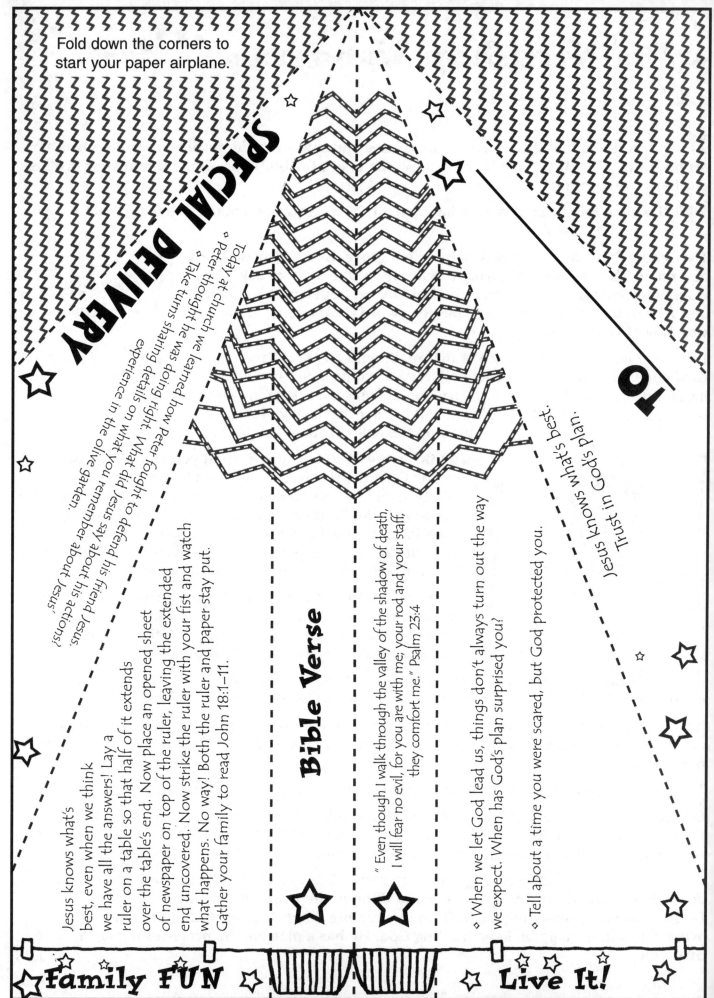

SPECIAL DELIVERY

TO

Today at church we learned how Peter fought to defend his friend Jesus. Peter thought he was doing right. What did Jesus say about his actions? Take turns sharing details on what you remember about Jesus in the olive garden.

Jesus knows what's best, even when we think we have all the answers! Lay a ruler on a table so that half of it extends over the table's end. Now place an opened sheet of newspaper on top of the ruler, leaving the extended end uncovered. Now strike the ruler with your fist and watch what happens. No way! Both the ruler and paper stay put. Gather your family to read John 18:1–11.

Bible Verse

" Even though I walk through the valley of the shadow of death, I will fear no evil, for you are with me; your rod and your staff, they comfort me." Psalm 23:4

◊ When we let God lead us, things don't always turn out the way we expect. When has God's plan surprised you?

◊ Tell about a time you were scared, but God protected you.

Jesus knows what's best.
Trust in God's plan.

Family FUN

Live It!

Easter Faith

Option

Get Set
LARGE GROUP ■ Greet kids and do a puppet skit. Schooner learns that a story can be both sad and happy.

❏ *large bird puppet* ❏ *puppeteer*

1

Bible 4U! Instant Drama
LARGE GROUP ■ Pilate, Peter and Mary tell about the events surrounding Jesus' death and resurrection.

3 actors ❏ *copies of pp. 120–121, Three Days that Changed Everything* ❏ *4 numbered balls. Optional:* ❏ *Bibletime costumes for Pilate, Peter and Mary*

2

Shepherd's Spot
SMALL GROUP ■ Use the "Faith Takes Off" handout to help kids proclaim their faith in Jesus, the risen Lord.

❏ *Bibles* ❏ *pencils* ❏ *scissors* ❏ *copies of p. 124, Faith Takes Off* ❏ *copies of p. 126, Special Delivery*

Option

Workshop Wonders
SMALL GROUP ■ Bake amazing "empty tomb" treats to celebrate the miracle of the resurrection.

❏ *large marshmallows* ❏ *refrigerated crescent dinner rolls* ❏ *bowl of melted margarine* ❏ *bowl of cinnamon and sugar* ❏ *small paper plates* ❏ *slotted spoons* ❏ *muffin pan*

Bible Basis
John 19:1-2, 6, 16–18; 20:1-16

Learn It!
Jesus rose from the dead for us.

Live It!
Put your faith in Jesus.

Bible Verse
I want to know Christ and the power of his resurrection. Philippians 3:10

Quick Takes

Then Pilate took Jesus and had him flogged. 2The soldiers twisted together a crown of thorns and put it on his head. They clothed him in a purple robe.

6As soon as the chief priests and their officials saw him, they shouted, "Crucify! Crucify!"

16–18 But Pilate answered, "You take him and crucify him. As for me, I find no basis for a charge against him." Finally Pilate handed him over to them to be crucified. So the soldiers took charge of Jesus. Carrying his own cross, he went out to the place of the Skull (which in Aramaic is called Golgotha). Here they crucified him, and with him two others—one on each side and Jesus in the middle.

20:1–16 Early on the first day of the week, while it was still dark, Mary Magdalene went to the tomb and saw that the stone had been removed from the entrance. So she came running to Simon Peter and the other disciple, the one Jesus loved, and said, "They have taken the Lord out of the tomb, and we don't know where they have put him!" So Peter and the other disciple started for the tomb. Both were running, but the other disciple outran Peter and reached the tomb first. He bent over and looked in at the strips of linen lying there but did not go in. Then Simon Peter, who was behind him, arrived and went into the tomb. He saw the strips of linen lying there, as well as the burial cloth that had been around Jesus' head. The cloth was folded up by itself, separate from the linen. Finally the other disciple, who had reached the tomb first, also went inside. He saw and believed. (They still did not understand from Scripture that Jesus had to rise from the dead.) Then the disciples went back to their homes, but Mary stood outside the tomb crying. As she wept, she bent over to look into the tomb and saw two angels in white, seated where Jesus' body had been, one at the head and the other at the foot. They asked her, "Woman, why are you crying?" "They have taken my Lord away," she said, "and I don't know where they have put him." At this, she turned round and saw Jesus standing there, but she did not realize that it was Jesus. "Woman," he said, "why are you crying? Who is it you are looking for?" Thinking he was the gardener, she said, "Sir, if you have carried him away, tell me where you have put him, and I will get him." Jesus said to her, "Mary." She turned towards him and cried out in Aramaic, "Rabboni!" (which means Teacher).

Insights

Three days changed everything. Jesus' brutal execution and triumphant resurrection opened a new way for sinful people to be restored to a loving relationship with God.

Pontius Pilate played an unwilling role in Jesus' execution. Judea was a small but troublesome Roman province. Pilate lived in Caesarea, but went down to Jerusalem during festivals to help keep the peace. Under Pilate's rule, Roman soldiers put down rebellions by both Jews and Samaritans. Riots and bloodshed brought negative attention from Caesar. Three times he tried to get the crowd to settle for a lesser punishment for Jesus; three times they demanded crucifixion. During the Passover feast, Jerusalem's population swelled with Jews from all over the known world. Pilate was not willing to risk the riot that seemed inevitable if he released Jesus, so he knowingly sent an innocent man to die.

Mary Magdalene plays a significant part in this story as well. She was the first to discover the empty tomb, and was also the first to see the risen Jesus. Jesus came to her as she wept by the empty tomb. "Mary," he said. In that tender moment she recognized his voice, and overwhelming grief turned to joy.

The events of these tumultuous days leave no room for ambivalence. Like Pilate, we all have to decide what to do with Jesus. Some of the children in your ministry still hold the simple, perfect trust of a young child. Others may be mature enough to realize that they can choose to believe and trust their lives to Jesus. Offer this lesson as a stepping stone to faith. Encourage your kids to believe that Jesus is the Son of God who died for them and who rose again to open the path to forgiveness and peace with God.

Option Get Set

Get kids warmed up with lively, interactive praise songs. **Hey—welcome everybody! You know, it makes my day to see this room full of your smiling faces. Now if I could just find that parrot...** *Schooner pops ups.*

Schooner: Hi, boss.

Leader: There you are, Schooner. Tell me, did you ever hear a Bible story that was both sad and happy?

Schooner: Sad and happy?

Leader: Sad and happy.

Schooner: Let me see if I can guess. It's about Jesus.

Leader: It is.

Schooner: He does something amazing—a great miracle.

Leader: Yep.

Schooner: I believe in miracles, boss.

Leader: I pretty much knew that already, Schooner.

Schooner: How?

Leader: A little birdie told me.

Schooner: That would be me! Jesus did so many cool things. The people just loved him.

Leader: Cries of love soon turned to cries of hate. People turned against Jesus and put him to death.

Schooner: *Squawk!* That can't be! You're pulling my leg.

Leader: It happened, Schooner.

Schooner: But...but...what about all the children Jesus helped? All those amazing miracles? People wouldn't hurt him.

Leader: Jesus was hurt for doing good things—for telling the world that he was the Son of God and that he could save them from their sins.

Schooner: *(shakes head)* I don't believe it, boss.

Leader: In today's Bible story, Jesus' life on earth comes to an end.

Schooner: *(sniff, sniff)* That's a very sad story.

Leader and Schooner: *(bow heads and sit in silence)*

Leader: But then his Father took care of things.

Schooner: *(excitedly)* Really?

Leader: Jesus did not stay dead. Jesus came back to life.

Schooner: Oh—I feel so much better!

Leader: Jesus is alive in heaven. And if we trust our lives to him, we'll go there to be with him some day.

Schooner: Woohoo! Now that's what I call a friend!

Leader: More than a friend, Schooner. He is our Savior.

Schooner: *(dances a little bird jig)* I'm so glad he rose from the dead.

Leader: So were his followers. In today's Bible story we're going to hear from them.

Schooner: Really? I can't wait!

Leader: Can you imagine how they felt when he died?

Schooner: (shakes his head) It must have been awful. If I'd been there, I'd have tucked my head under my wing and never come out.

Leader: They were really sad, and scared too.

Schooner: Then everything changed!

Leader: It sure did. And nothing's been the same ever since!

Schooner: How did they find out Jesus was alive?

Leader: You don't want me to give away the Bible story, do you?

Schooner: I suppose not. But can we hurry up and get on with it?

Leader: Sure thing, Schooner. Next up—Bible 4U!

Bible 4U!

It's amazing how things can change in just a few days. On Sunday, everyone welcomed Jesus to Jerusalem with palm branches and shouts of "Hosanna!" On Thursday night they arrested him, and on Friday they put him to death.

It was the week of the Passover feast, so Jerusalem was full of visitors. The religious leaders spread lies about Jesus all week. They could arrest him, but they couldn't put him to death. Only the Roman governor could do that. So they brought him to Pilate and demanded that he be crucified. When Jesus died, darkness covered the sky and the earth shook.

Jesus' followers were terrified. This man who had brought love and healing to so many people was dead. They didn't know that God's plan was only half finished. Soon it would be Sunday—how things would change!

Let's hear this story from three people who were there. Pontius Pilate, the Roman governor will tell his story first. Then we'll hear from two of Jesus' closest friends, Peter and Mary Magdalene. We'll begin on Friday of the week that changed everything.

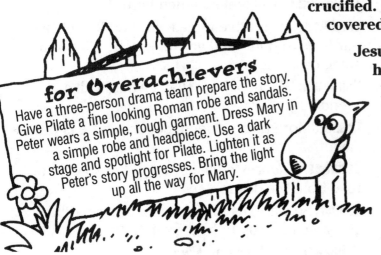

Three Days that Changed Everything
Based on John 19:1–2, 6, 16–18; 20:1–8.

Pilate enters.

That whole thing with Jesus of Nazareth that happened last Friday—I just can't get it out of my mind. The Jews brought him to me and wanted me to crucify him. I'm Pontius Pilate, the governor of Judea. The Jewish court didn't have the power to put him to death. So they wanted me to order it.

I questioned Jesus myself. The man hadn't done anything wrong! I thought if I had Jesus beaten, it would be enough to satisfy the crowd. But they chanted, "Crucify him! Crucify him!" If I didn't go along with them, there would have been a riot. The city would have exploded with violence—

I don't know if my soldiers could have kept control.

My wife had a dream about Jesus. She knew he was innocent. She sent me a message and warned me not to have anything to do with him. But what could I do? The crowd would not be satisfied with anything but his death, so I finally let them take Jesus to be crucified.

Pilate exits.

Peter enters.

My head is still spinning. I just can't seem to take in everything that's happened during the last four days. It started when we were in the garden. I was tired, everything was quiet, and Jesus had gone off by himself to pray. Then there were soldiers with torches and spears. When they arrested Jesus I tried to fight, but he told me to put my sword away.

I followed in the cold darkness. They took him to the high priest's house. I could see them questioning him. A servant girl asked me if I had been with Jesus. I said no—three times! Then a cock crowed and I remembered that Jesus had told me I would deny him. I ran away and cried.

Then they crucified him. It didn't seem possible that this could happen, but it did. He died on a cross. Some of our friends took his body to a tomb. All my hope died with him that awful Friday.

Early Sunday morning Mary went to put spices on his body. She came running back from the tomb, shouting, "They have taken our Lord and I don't know where they've put him!" John and I ran to the tomb to see for ourselves. The great stone that covered the entrance had been rolled away! I went into the tomb. The cloths they had wrapped him in were there, but he wasn't. Then I knew—he had risen—from the dead!

Peter exits.

Mary enters.

When they took Jesus down from the cross, I wanted to take care of his body. But it was too late. The Sabbath had begun, so our friends just laid him in a tomb. Pilate ordered soldiers to stand guard. And they put a huge stone in front of the tomb.

Early Sunday morning I gathered spices and oils and went to the tomb to take care of Jesus' body. The stone was gone and the tomb was empty! I didn't

know what to think. I went running back to the house where the disciples were staying. Peter and John came back to the tomb with me. They could see he was gone. I couldn't believe it! I missed him so much.

Peter and John went back to the house, but I stayed at the tomb. I looked in once more, and there were two angels in white sitting where Jesus' body had been. They asked, "Woman, why are you crying?"

I answered, "They have taken my Lord away." Then I realized there was someone behind me. At first I thought it was the gardener. He asked me why I was I crying. I begged him to tell me where he had put Jesus.

Then he said my name. His voice was so kind. I knew that voice—it was Jesus! My teacher! He was alive and standing right in front of me. He knew my name. It was my Lord, risen from the dead.

He told me to go tell the disciples. My legs couldn't carry me fast enough. I was running, laughing, crying, stumbling all the way back to the house. You should have seen their faces when I told them Jesus was alive. They wanted to believe me. They hoped it was true, but they weren't sure.

I'm here to tell you it's true. Jesus died and rose from the dead. He talked to me in that tender, loving voice that I remembered. I thought everything was lost. I thought there was no hope. But Jesus came back to us. He came back for us. If we believe and trust him as Savior, we'll go to be with him in heaven.

Jesus is alive. He loves you. He knows your name, too. He invites you to believe in him—to accept the love and forgiveness he offers.

HE'S ALIVE!

Mary exits.

Wow! That's an amazing story. And it's not just a story—it's absolutely true. It's something God planned from the beginning of time. Let's see if you caught what happened.

Toss the four numbered balls to different parts of the room. Bring the kids with the balls to the front one-by-one and ask these questions. Allow kids to get help from the group if they need it. After each correct answer, let kids drop the ball into a bag.

 ■ **Pilate knew Jesus hadn't done anything wrong. Why did he let Jesus be crucified?**

 ■ **If you could have given Pilate advice, what would you have said?**

 ■ **How did Mary know it was Jesus who was talking to her?**

 ■ **Why did Jesus die and rise again?**

God created people so we could worship him and love him with all our hearts. Way back in the Garden of Eden when Adam and Eve sinned, they broke the friendship between God and his people. Someone needed to pay for that sin. That someone was Jesus.

He came to earth as a baby, grew up and taught people about God. And then he died willingly so our sins could be forgiven. On the cross, he took the punishment for all the wrong things people have done. That includes you and me. He invites us to put our faith in him, to ask him to forgive our sins, and to be his followers.

Jesus' forgiveness makes us clean inside. He promises to be our friend and helper, and to fill our hearts with his love.

Today in your shepherd groups you'll discover what it means to put your faith in Jesus.

Dismiss kids to their shepherd groups.

Bible Verse
I want to know Christ and the power of his resurrection. Philippians 3:10

2 Shepherd's Spot

Gather your small group and help kids find John 19 in their Bibles.

The first four books of the New Testament are Matthew, Mark, Luke and John. We call them the Gospels. They tell the story of Jesus' life. Matthew, Mark, Luke and John all tell about Jesus' death and resurrection. Today we're going to look at John's story. Because it's a long story, we'll pick out some verses to read.

Have volunteers take turns reading these passages aloud: John 19:1–2, 6, 16–18; 20:1–8.

When Jesus died his friends and disciples felt like it was the end of everything good. They were sad and scared. When they realized he had risen, they didn't know what to think at first. Would they believe he could really do that?

■ **Share a time you felt sad, then something changed and you were suddenly wonderfully happy.**

Later Jesus appeared to them and talked with them. They began to understand, and they put their faith in Jesus. They trusted everything he told them. That's called "faith." When we have faith, we step up and say, "I believe in you, Jesus. I trust you, and I want you to be my Lord."

Today's project is called "Faith Takes Off." It's a butterfly that's just taking flight. I hope today's story will help your faith take off!

Distribute the "Faith Takes Off" handout (p. 124) and lead kids through the assembly instructions.

1. Cut out the butterfly and the base.
2. Make a mountain fold in the center of the butterfly.
3. Make valley folds where the wings attach to the body.
4. Make valley folds at the tail.
5. Spread the tail and glue it to the base.

Ask a volunteer to read Philippians 3:10 from the base.

If you want to know the power of Jesus' resurrection, sign your initials somewhere on the base. Then take it home and invite your family members to initial it too.

Invite kids to share their concerns, then close with prayer.
Dear Jesus, we know you did something no one else has ever done. You died on the cross for us, then rose from the dead. Help our faith in you "take off" as we celebrate the joy of knowing you're alive today. Please hear our prayers for (mention kids' requests). **We praise you as our living Lord, amen!**

Faith Takes Off

1. Cut out the butterfly and the base.
2. Make a mountain fold in the center of the butterfly.
3. Make valley folds where the wings attach to the body.
4. Make valley folds at the tail.
5. Spread the tail and glue it to the shaded triangles on the base.

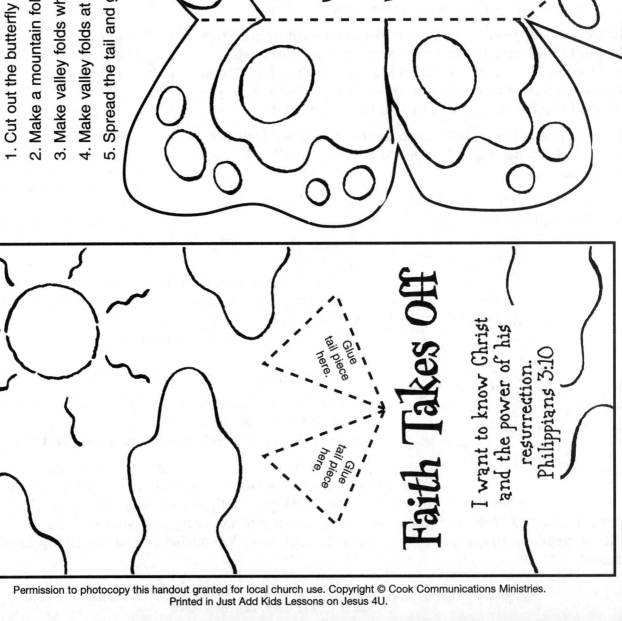

Glue tail piece here.

Glue tail piece here.

Faith Takes Off

I want to know Christ and the power of his resurrection. Philippians 3:10

Option Workshop Wonders

Get List:
- ❏ large marshmallows
- ❏ refrigerated crescent dinner rolls
- ❏ bowl of melted margarine (1/4 cup)
- ❏ bowl of cinnamon and sugar
- ❏ small paper plates
- ❏ slotted spoons
- ❏ muffin pan

Joy in the morning! After a lonely and painful death for our sins, the body of Jesus was placed in a cave tomb by loving and tearful friends. But Jesus would not stay there long. God raised his Son, Jesus, so we might have life in him forever. Jesus knows each of us by name and invites us to put our faith in him.

Have enough crescent rolls and plates for the kids in your class. Give kids a chance to wash their hands thoroughly. Then let them each take a dough triangle and a marshmallow and place both on a plate.

Your dough will represent the tomb where Jesus was buried. We'll place a marshmallow inside the tomb to represent Jesus' body. Have kids take turns dipping their marshmallows into the melted margarine, then rolling it in cinnamon and sugar. **The cinnamon and sugar are like the spices that his friends came to place on his body.** Pause as kids work.

Finally, say, **Place your marshmallow on the short end of your crescent and roll it up. Be sure to pinch the dough closed, to seal the "tomb."** Pass around a muffin pan and let kids drop in their rolls. Place the pan in an oven set at 375º and bake them for about 10 minutes, or until they're lightly browned. Have kids hang on to their plates.

As the rolls bake, talk about:

■ **What difference does it make to you that Jesus rose from the dead?**

■ **If you were going to talk to someone who had never heard about Jesus before, what would you say?**

■ **What happens when we ask Jesus to forgive us and fill our hearts with his love?**

Mmm. I smell something good. Remove the rolls from the oven, place them on kids' plates and let them cool. **The tomb could not hold Jesus. Not even the huge stone and the Roman soldiers could keep him there. God raised him from the dead!**

■ **Where is Jesus right now?**

Let's see what has happened to our rolls. Invite kids to take a bite. **Surprise! The "tomb" is empty! Just like Jesus said it would be. Jesus has risen. Allelulia!**

Remember the empty tomb this week. Jesus is alive and he lives in us!

Option: If you prefer, have kids flatten plain biscuit dough in the palms of their hands, drop marshmallows into the center of the dough, pull dough up and pinch closed. Drop dough "tombs" into a muffin tin. Sprinkle sugar mixture on top and bake.

Fold down the corners to start your paper airplane.

SPECIAL DELIVERY

TO

Today at church we learned that Jesus died and rose again. We can put our faith in him.

○ What does it mean to trust in Jesus?

○ How have you seen Jesus' "resurrection power" at work in your life?

Put your faith in Jesus.

Bible Verse

"I want to know Christ and the power of his resurrection."
Philippians 3:10

Make an Easter snack using warm, snack-size soft tortillas. Use kitchen scissors to cut out shapes from today's story: a cross, tomb circles, angels or the figures of Mary Magdalene, Peter or the risen Jesus. Metal cookie cutters would work well for people shapes. Spray both sides of the cut tortilla with vegetable oil, sprinkle on some Parmesan cheese, and set on a cookie sheet. Bake in a 350° oven for six minutes. Cool. Serve with your favorite dip and share the joy of the risen Savior!

◇ What do you believe happens when people die?

◇ Some people celebrate two birthdays. The day of their birth and the day they accepted Jesus into their hearts. Which do you celebrate?

◇ On a "power" scale of 1 to 10 how powerful is Jesus rising from the dead?

Family FUN

Live It!